WHAT WE ARE ABOUT TO RECEIVE

WHAT
WE ARE ABOUT
TO RECEIVE

BY

JOHN FRANKLIN CARTER
(JAY FRANKLIN, pseud.)

Essay Index Reprint Series

BOOKS FOR LIBRARIES PRESS
FREEPORT, NEW YORK

First Published 1932
Reprinted 1968

LIBRARY OF CONGRESS CATALOG CARD NUMBER:

68-29196

PRINTED IN THE UNITED STATES OF AMERICA

E
805
.C 26
1968

TO THAT ASTUTE UNOFFICIAL OBSERVER
S.C.

CONTENTS

WHAT WE ARE ABOUT TO RECEIVE

For what we are about to receive
may the Lord make us truly thankful

I

Our Next President?

PRESIDENT HOOVER stands right on the "X" which marks the spot where the election of 1932 will occur. He is determined to succeed himself, come what may, and prove to the country that his name need not go down to history as the synonym of national distress. He is the biggest issue of the election. Some of the Democrats say they need no other issue, no platform, not even a candidate—just the name "Herbert Hoover"—to sweep the country. Some of the Republicans pretend that he is a man of sad and lonely strength, a sort of tragic demigod doomed to suffer in silence for the sins of the American people. Most of us merely see a serious and isolated man, who means well, tries hard, and is doing his utmost to serve the country in his own way. A humorless and earnest figure who deserves better luck and, with that luck, might go down to history as one of our abler leaders.

Whatever the facts are, Herbert Hoover is himself. He does not pretend to be a hero, saint, or second Lincoln. He is neither an imitation Roosevelt nor a synthetic Wilson. He may or may not be a good President, a great man, or even a good engineer, but he acts and talks like no one else on earth, and does not hesitate to follow his own line, against all advice and all indications of public opinion.

This is damnable in the eyes of those who wish to stampede him into action. As a result, he is one of the best-cursed men in public life and, if the theory that every knock is a boost holds true of politics, he should be re-elected in a walk-over in November 1932. Unfortunately, abuse after a certain point fails to help a public man, mud does stick—which is why politicians use it—public opinion, once estranged, is like a faithless wife—never quite the same.

As for his temperamental fitness for the job of Chief Executive of this exciting Republic, there is a difference of opinion among our political crooners, but the rank and file will remain indifferent to the nicer points of political taxidermy. He is slow and stubborn in an age which likes boldness and energy. He is so thin-skinned that, like many of our public men, he tends to regard all hostile criticism as inspired by the Evil One and so allows himself to be drawn into stupid little brawls with those who oppose his policies. He is Constitutional in an age which is getting pretty tired of the Constitution. He is lacking in political sex appeal. He has not that "It" which marks a great leader, and his followers must take him with their eyes open and their mouths shut. He is as undramatic as a porcelain bathtub, as unspectacular as a cash register, as unmagnetic as a telegraph pole—but, like all of these articles, he is extremely useful and practically inevitable.

He will be the candidate of the Republican Party, bar death or revolution. And whoever votes for him will do so with resignation, desperation, hope, confidence or by force of habit, but entirely without enthusiasm.

He will make a fairly good candidate as he is adept in evading issues and, in an election year, "issues" are simply irrelevant means by which the opposition converts prejudice into votes. He will have behind him the record of three and a half tough years as President during the world's greatest depression, in which he contrived to keep his head, do nothing foolish, and maintain the political principles for which he stood in 1928: individual liberty within the law (including the Prohibition law) and collective action to promote national rather than individual welfare. It's Victorian stuff, of course, a little musty and a damn sight too legalistic to satisfy people in a hurry, but it is in the American tradition.

His opponents will challenge him to debate Prohibition, unemployment, farm relief, tariff reduction, water power, and foreign policy. He will leave them to his Party's sandbaggers and will talk blandly—and at reasonable length—about peace, prosperity and American ideals. He will not only refuse to fight; he will also refuse to run away; and he will depend upon the morale and momentum of his Party and the sense of the American people to vindicate him and all his works.

WHAT WE ARE ABOUT TO RECEIVE

Although this is excellent political strategy, he is a poor Party politician. He has never grasped the principle of "divide and rule" as applied to the Congressional rough and tumble. He lets his enemies gang up on him and then directs his political tactics at their strongest, rather than at their weakest, point. He is convicted of the unforgivable sin of Party politics—ingratitude—as one after another of the men and women who secured his nomination and election in 1928 has been forced to walk the plank, out of national politics and out of public life. That's bad for the morale of his Party, which follows him now largely because failure to do so would reveal its own political bankruptcy. He is hated by the Senate, has no control of his Party in the House and the elections of 1930 and 1931 have wiped out his Party's majority and have indicated that the tide of political opinion is against him.

As a statesman, he is anybody's guess. He lacks the divine gift of leadership. He works too far in the background and too close to business fundamentals to tickle the more moral fancies of the American people. He is patient and optimistic—two excellent qualities in a public man—and yet strangely irritable in his approach to particular political problems. He is reported to prefer "Yes Men" around him and is impatient of disagreement. He has not understood that leadership in a democracy involves the knack of suffering fools gladly. He does not appear to realize that, even though at times it is best to do nothing, it is necessary to appear to be doing something. He lacks showmanship. During the great depression he has acted more like the general who does not hesitate to sacrifice his troops to win a position than like the compassionate father of his country, whose heart must break loudly and publicly for the sufferings of his poor people.

His record in office is sound without being exciting. His chief mistakes have been the signature of a neolithic tariff, the national neglect of the national problem of unemployment, the evasion of the Prohibition problem, and the steady weakening of our naval defense. His chief achievements have been the creation of the Federal Farm Board, the naval agreement with England and Japan, the moratorium on war debts and reparations, the utilization of the world's peace machinery to promote American policy in Manchuria, the stabilization of our financial machinery, and the staving off of a dole and bonus grab from the Federal Treasury.

President Hoover goes into the campaign with lukewarm supporters and vigorous opponents. The farmers who elected him in 1928 have had two years of low prices, foreclosures and destitution. Despite the up-turn in the wheat market in the Fall of 1931, there is no guarantee that they will have recovered their world markets in 1932. The farm vote cannot be counted upon in the Presidential sweepstakes. The Prohibitionists are strong for him, but they represent a losing cause and there will be no Catholic issue to line up Protestant votes for him this year. The Native Americans are still for him, in theory, but in practice they are mostly in the sunny South where Republican votes don't count. The big bankers are more or less for him, but unless he can secure their foreign investments by cancelling the war debts and lowering the tariff, they won't stick to him. The big manufacturers and the railroads should be for him, but the railroads have lost their fight for an increase in rates and the manufacturers have lost so much money that they'll fall for any Party which promises them a miraculous return to Coolidge Prosperity—and Hoover is too honest to promise that to any one.

Against him are ranged the reactionary bosses of the Democratic Solid South, that section of the country which has not produced an outstanding political leader or idea since the Civil War. The Liberals of the North and the Progressives of the West detest him. The "wets" no longer pretend to believe that he is not a thorough "dry." The Catholics, on the whole, are neutral, but the Catholic vote tends to follow the foreign vote and the foreign vote is mostly wet. The foreign vote, by reason of thirst, religion and opposition to the native sons, tends to the Democratic side and eight million unemployed and the twenty million impoverished Americans are being taught to regard Hoover as responsible for all their troubles. The popular odds are all against him.

His record can be played to almost any tune which

8

the rabble-rousers desire to call and most people, so far as they think politically, believe that the sequence of events is a clear proof of cause and effect. We elected Hoover in 1928 and we had a panic in 1929 and a depression ever since. We elected Hoover in 1928 and in 1931 we were deeply involved in European politics and had our representative sitting on the Council of the League of Nations. We elected Hoover in 1928 and now, for the first time in nearly forty years, we have serious social unrest and the growth of revolutionary sentiment. We also have the ghastly mess of Prohibition and the worst farm crisis since the 'Nineties. This is what Hoover has cost the country in the eyes of all simple people who believe that a President has all but supernatural powers over the behavior of the human race.

What can he offer the country to offset this demagogic indictment? Long-range economic wisdom may be on his side, but an election is a short-range affair. His policy may be leading America to world power without danger of downfall, but you can't eat world power if you're hungry, you can't pay rent with it if you're broke, it doesn't give you a job. The restoration of local self-government may be inherent in all of his domestic policies and the stressing of the value of individual initiative may be necessary to prevent social dry rot in an age which clamors to let George do it, but local politics can't solve urgent national problems quickly and rugged individualism is at a discount in an age of machinery. When people are starving or have been turned out of their homes, they don't give a damn for what is Constitutional and best for everybody in the long run. You can die, in the short run.

His whole policy is too damn stodgy to appeal to the voters or to inspire them to solve their own problems. On Prohibition, he is a dry politically, but not a fanatic, personally. He opposes the dole and prefers charity as a means of relieving economic distress. He made his reputation as an administrator of charity. He believes that each community should look after its own unemployed, not pass the buck to Washington. He believes in the private operation of business, including public utilities. He wants to settle social unrest by creating a nation of home-owning and home-loving families who will pay off their mortgages and be content with things as they are. His program for Farm Relief is to lend the farm organizations Federal funds to enable them to organize and improve their business methods, not to give the individual farmer enough cash to enable him to avoid the consequences of economic inefficiency. He believes that the Tariff can be slowly modified by scientific procedure and that, in the meantime, the push it has given to foreign tariffs is moving the world on towards a more sensible organization of its economic life. In short, Herbert Hoover is essentially a middle-class man with an excellent middle-class mind and a solid, stolid middle-class policy.

And he has started more things moving internationally than any American leader since Wilson. His tariff is leading to a new economic alignment of Europe and the British Empire. His moratorium has started a diplomatic free-for-all in Europe that may lead to a complete revision of the peace treaties. He has started the United States on the road to socialism, through his farm and bank policies. His peace and disarmament policies are leading to a revision of the political map of Asia and to a reorganization of power in Europe. His panic—if it *was* his—has led to the financial co-operation of France and America to maintain the gold standard against the world.

If re-elected, he may push through some of the things which he has started, but he cannot do much harm or good. No one man can. He can perhaps move his country a little closer to a new social and economic order, based upon American traditions in politics and upon capitalistic organization in economics. He can perhaps move the world a little closer to a new organization of its power and resources, based on diplomatic co-operation and international finance. He may be able to shift finance a little from purely private and speculative channels in the direction of political and social progress. That's not much, but it might be worth having.

His chance of securing the Republican nomination is unexcelled. He controls the party machinery, the delegates, the jobs with which to bribe the bosses, the publicity with which to dope the rank and file. His chances of being elected are perfectly rotten, judged by the usual standards. Neither his own Party nor his former supporters have the slightest personal enthusiasm for him, no matter what their confidence in his ability. The country has thought it has suffered too much in the last three years for him to count on wide popularity, if it is true that the voters always back the man who promises them everything and kick the man who costs them money. Not once in a century has the President of a panic year been re-elected. Moreover, the country has had the Republicans in power for twelve years and is getting bored with them on general principles. The politicians are against him and the demagogues are already dancing on his political grave.

His only chance of breaking the charm and retaining office must lie beyond the normal calculations of politics. With the *mechanical* odds against him, he can be saved only by a sort of *chemical* change in the electorate—something like the overwhelming victory of the National Government in Great Britain—an appeal to the darkest fears and purest patriotism of the American people. He must somehow manage to make the campaign a struggle, not between two parties, but between the United States and revolution, between Good and Evil. To get four more years in the White House, he must frighten the nation out of seven years' growth. He can embark on a second term only if he is prepared to use the Stars and Stripes, the Ten Commandments and the American Constitution as a gangplank. Some of us believe that he is too honest and too big a man to pay that price for re-election.

II

Another Roosevelt in the White House?

FRANKLIN DELANO ROOSEVELT, Harvard graduate,
Governor of the State of New York, and gentleman,
is the best bet in the race for the Democratic presidential
nomination. He is an irrepressible candidate. Scarcely a
day goes by or an issue bobs up but Roosevelt hits the
front page with a statement or something. He issues as
many statements as there are issues, and strokes backs
indefatigably until he dominates Democratic thought
as the "logical candidate." Whether it is a straw vote or
a wet debate, the name of Roosevelt appears like magic
and his availability has rolled up into a sizable snowball
of political popularity.

In all this, he has revealed himself as a consummate
politician. He has inherited Al Smith's uncanny knack
of making a Republican legislature play Democratic
tunes. He has built up the Democratic Party in the
Upper New York State districts where the Republicans
have for generations voted the full strength of the grave-
yards and the orphan asylums to pile up "record ma-
jorities." He has erased the Tammany taint from his candidacy by helping to investigate the corruption in New

York City, and has even gone so far that he out-maneuvered Al Smith on the reforestation policy, thereby proving that from now until Election Day, New York Democrats must carry the Roosevelt brand. He picked up friends and delegates in every state of the Union until the only question was whether he would go into the nomination convention with a two-thirds majority. That man knows politics.

That does not mean that he will make a good candidate. On the contrary, he will make a rather poor one— but in 1932 the Democrats may not need anything more to win. He is an invalid, a point which will seriously affect his appeal to the voters. It does not matter that he has made a courageous comeback from infantile paralysis or that he is the liveliest cripple in American politics. When a candidate appears with crutches and a wheelchair, the haunting suspicion arises that he will not be able to stand the strain of the White House. The doctors say that he could, but the White House has killed strong men. Then again, Roosevelt is a gentleman, which is always a slight handicap in our public life. The grimy boys with hair on their chests resent the idea that a man can get along without vulgarity. Roosevelt will not measure up to the standard of political horseplay and has too much humor to engage in the solemn tub-thumping which passes for moral sincerity in the crossroads regions of the United States. And finally, there is a widespread conviction that Franklin Roosevelt lacks guts, that he can't force the pace or take punishment, and that when cornered he will play dead dog. He is not a fighter.

If he gets into the White House, it will be as a blank cheque. Nobody has the slightest idea of whether he is "another Roosevelt" or just another Democratic candidate. No one knows whether he is a statesman or a name. There is much to be said for the novel idea of putting a politician in the White House, after our depressing experiences with an engineer, a college professor and a judge in that august residence, but politicians can degenerate into wire-pullers, and a weak politician can do almost as much harm as a well-meaning plumber in national politics. If Roosevelt becomes President we will have to take him pretty much on faith.

His record is of little help in sizing up this charming and adroit gentleman who has staged the gamest comeback in our recent political history. In 1920 he was his party's candidate for vice president and he went down in the terrible Harding landslide that put the Ohio gang in power and the League of Nations in cold storage. Before that, Roosevelt had been an able Assistant Secretary of the Navy during the War and had taken the curse of Josephus Daniels off the administration of the fleet. After the fatal election, Roosevelt collapsed with infantile paralysis—a fate which usually overtakes successful candidates—and has never fully recovered. He maintained touch with politics, however, putting Al Smith's name in nomination at the Democratic Conventions of 1924 and

WHAT WE ARE ABOUT TO RECEIVE

1928. In that terrible year of the Hoover landslide, Smith drafted Roosevelt to run for the governorship of New York. Roosevelt carried the state when Smith lost it, and carried it again in 1930. Hence his availability. New York State is worth carrying and it is worth being carried by New York, if you have Presidential ambitions.

Thus it is that Roosevelt is far out in front. Unfortunately, that is the most definite thing that can be said about him. With two years of depression in which to make hay of Hoover's unpopularity, Roosevelt is still cheerfully vague on all the issues and ideas on which men can be brought to fight or to vote. His availability for the Democratic nomination is the sum and substance of his record as Governor of New York.

This is not to his discredit. Things have come to a pretty pass when a big governorship marks the end of a man's ambitions. The point is that New York State will have to pay a price for the Roosevelt candidacy. The citizens of the State will have to face a heavy increase in taxation in order that the state's unemployed may receive help at the instance of Governor Roosevelt. The water-power question in New York has been worked into the presidential pattern and the St. Lawrence waterway project—which won't be completed for years and years and which hasn't even been started—was used by Roosevelt as a stalking horse for an attack upon Hoover's position on the national aspects of the power question. For too long a time Roosevelt temporized with the stench of Tammany corruption and then went only far enough to placate the anti-Tammany feeling in the south and west. He could so easily have pushed for a concurrent investigation of the corruption in some of New York State's Republican cities, that one suspects him of having played politics or traded votes on the whole nauseating problem of city government in an age which has the "gimmes" in politics and the heebie-jeebies in economics.

Set against this is a record of some really liberal and progressive legislation. Thanks to Franklin Roosevelt, New York has old age pensions. Thanks to Roosevelt, New York is grappling with the problem of unemployment insurance at a time when the Federal Government acts as though a series of low growls at Russia and the deportation of a few minor members of the Communist Party were the final solution of the greatest problem of our age. There is no doubt that Roosevelt's heart is in the right place and that he views the spectacle of human suffering in an industrial democracy as demanding action rather than optimistic hand-outs. In spite of his patrician upbringing and Harvard education, he reveals greater readiness to regard unemployment as something more than a difficult statistical problem than does Herbert Hoover, whose life was a series of hard knocks. In fact, Roosevelt's record shows pretty clearly that there is much more in common between the rich and the poor than there is between the poor and the ex-poor. The self-made man is always a harder boss than is the aristocrat, and Roosevelt represents the all but forgotten strain of chivalry, untempered by self-righteous morality, in the tradition of our public life. Theodore Roosevelt had it, with much the same background, when he championed the striking anthracite miners against the coal barons at a time when a strike was regarded as akin to treason and property rights as having been established by Jehovah.

It would be a pleasant change to have men regarded as human beings rather than statistics.

That is why we wish that Franklin Roosevelt weren't so vague whenever he meets an issue. We are looking for a chance to admire him as well as like him. He's all so transparent and pinkish—like jello—and just about as exhilarating. On the subject of Prohibition, he is mildly wet but not so wet as to lose the vote of Bishop Cannon's friends. He agrees with Hoover on unemployment relief in practice—that the problem is up to the local communities and then the states—but for public consumption he tries to give the unemployed the impression that he favors the dole, at the same time persuading the bankers that he is fundamentally sound. He has made a sort of sulky virtue out of the fact that the state should relieve distress before the Federal government can be asked to foot the bills. His water-power policy is equally two-sided. He believes that the state should control production but that private business should control distribution of hydro-electric power. In other words, the taxpayers shall foot the heavy costs of investment and the private interests shall secure the profits. This is an unfair distortion of the Roosevelt theory, which presupposes that by controlling production the state can control prices to the consumer. Anyone who knows politics and business, however, knows that in practice it will not work out long that way.

On every other issue—tariff, farm relief, disarmament, foreign policy, banking policy, social unrest—he is as hard to pin down as a live eel on a sheet of oilcloth. These issues aren't his chickens and he won't hatch those eggs until he comes to them. Just the same, the whole impression which he gives is one of gentlemanly opportunism, reluctance to take a position or to follow a policy which might lose him a vote or offend an ally. It's hard to serve two masters and it's hard to be governor of a big state and also a long-distance Presidential candidate.

If he makes the race he will be handicapped by the fact that he has many friends and few foes. He is supported with restrained enthusiasm by the wets, while the drys refrain from political hydrophobia when his name is mentioned. The Liberals and Progressives will be fairly strong for him, though they couldn't be held in line against a really progressive candidate like Borah. At the same time Wall Street likes him. And Roosevelt's greatest asset at the present time is the support of Colonel House. That wily old Texan picked Wilson and he has now picked Roosevelt—to win. House knows every trick of the game, national and international, and he can give Roosevelt the sort of advice which every President ought to get and which so few of them listen to when they can get it.

Colonel House is playing to bring over to Roosevelt the vote of protest against hard times. The rebound from the Hoover landslide has been terrific. In the first year after the election of 1928, the Solid South hounded out of public life all the Hoovercrats who had broken the Democratic ranks and had given a Republican candidate electoral votes in the lynching belt. At the election of 1930 and 1931, the Republicans were put definitely on the defensive for the first time since 1916. Higher prices for wheat and signs of life in the stock ticker may take the curse off the Republicans before the elections of 1932, but it's not worth gambling on now. Unless a few political miracles materialize before November, it will be the sort of year in which the Democrats could nominate a yellow dog. If you add the votes of those who feel fooled by Hoover to the votes of the Solid South, pour in the funds of the very biggest bankers who think that Hoover is too damn socialistic, and season with the Catholic and immigrant hangover votes from 1928, you have all the ingredients of a Roosevelt landslide in 1932.

The embarrassing thing about this simple little problem in political algebra is that Roosevelt has no foes. That is his greatest weakness. No one can respect him for the enemies he has made, for he has made no enemies.

And yet we all know that millions of people, including many who have suffered like the very devil from this stupid depression, will vote against Roosevelt and for Hoover.

Why? Party loyalty and party habit isn't the only explanation. There is the fact that Roosevelt appears to be on the make politically, a man who stands for nothing very solid himself and who does nothing which might injure his chances of being nominated. It is not enough to answer that Hoover is another opportunist and that he is an unsuccessful one. He may be, but he gives the appearance of sincerity and he does stand very definitely for several distinctly unpopular things. Wilson did, too, for that matter, and Wilson himself was never defeated in a political campaign. Roosevelt, as yet, has not dared to take an unpopular course. Until he does we will not know whether he stands a real chance of making a victorious party of all the millions who yearn for a conspicuously liberal and energetic leader.

If Roosevelt were elected he would make a good President. He has charm, education, training in public life, and good breeding. He is clever politically and able administratively. He would avoid unnecessary personal friction and would be, in some ways, a second Wilson. He could bring the country a little closer to liberalism in its social ideas and to progress in its political institutions. He could facilitate American co-operation in the financial reorganization of the world by lower tariffs and debt cancellation. He might recognize Russia or bring us into the League of Nations or build a larger navy or start a fresh series of interventions in Latin America. He could give a thorough house-cleaning to the moth-eaten and musty administration of the national government. He could inaugurate that overdue era of reform which had to be laid aside in camphor in 1916, when we saw that we would have to go to war with Germany and could not afford the time or energy to reorganize our society on a decent political and economic basis. Roosevelt could give the country a sane, cheerful and kind-hearted administration and actually do a lot of good in the process.

His chances of being nominated are better than those of any other Democrat. His chances of being elected, if nominated, are so good that the Republicans will have to invent some brand-new political strategy—on the order of tanks or poison gas—to stop him.

His chances of going down in history as a great statesman are not promising. So few of our Presidents have done so.

On the other hand, Franklin Roosevelt in the White House might go down in history as one of our most attractive and sensible leaders. He is an aristocrat, with an aristocratic mind and an aristocratic policy. That means that his mind is open, skeptical, and can be changed without requiring the complete moral reorganization of the universe or a special visitation from the Holy Ghost. It means that his policy will be one of readiness to do the necessary and honorable thing, promptly and cheerfully, without referring it to a commission, preparing blue-prints, or charting its progress from factory to con-sumer. It means that in Roosevelt we would have an undogmatic, light-hearted and straightforward gentle-man in the White House, and that his successes and his failures would be those of a man trained to self-control, sportsmanship and consideration for others as the foun-dation of private and public life.

Another Roosevelt in the White House might not give us the heavyweight, hard-boiled type of plunging policy which we may need in the next few years, but neither would he give us the mournful and all but maudlin type of soft-headed and soft-hearted policy which is the aim of our multitudinous idealists and professors. In an age in which we must keep our balance and maintain our national interests without truculence or cringing, we could do far worse than elect as President a man who has been brought up to believe that privileges confer obligations and that life is not so serious that one can afford not to act like a gentleman.

III

The Political Resurrection of Al Smith

EIGHT years ago, Alfred Emmanuel Smith, wet, Governor of New York State, Tammany politician, wearer of the brown derby and product of the East Side and the Fulton Fish Market, strove for the Democratic nomination. In the Madison Square Garden Convention he was brought to a standstill by William Gibbs McAdoo and yielded to a compromise candidate who was easily beaten by Calvin Coolidge. Four years ago the same Al Smith—McAdoo being out—was nominated by the Democratic Convention at Houston, Texas. The brown derby became a symbol of the revolt of the city-bred, the aliens, and the wets against the smug and complacent forces of the dry countryside. He made a game campaign and was shatteringly defeated by Herbert Hoover, though he had won nearly six million more votes than had ever been cast for a Democratic Presidential candidate.

It seemed to be the end. Al Smith was through. Now, four years after Herbert Hoover crushed him in the most dreadful political defeat the Democrats had suffered in fifty years, Al Smith has lifted his head and has refused to admit that he is a Presidential has-been. On February 8, he published an "I might choose to run" statement which has made him available for the Democratic nomination, after months of sitting on the fence, while his friend, Franklin Roosevelt, was headed for the nomination. The statement, backed by the memory of Smith's sixteen million votes in 1928, has proved a political bombshell. The "Block Roosevelt" movement has come to life with a vengeance and the Hoover Republicans have cheered up for the first time since Nick Longworth died, while the southern and western Democrats are looking anxiously to their lines of communication. The old brown derby is no longer Smith's political tombstone and the man who played the part of the corpse at the big wake of 1928 may be leading the political parade in 1932. Not since Bryan came back after his fatal Free Silver campaign of 1896, to give the Democratic Party two more personally conducted tours to political defeat, has America seen anything quite like it.

The political resurrection of Al Smith is the most important event in recent national politics and will wreck more political plans than would be smashed by the sudden return of Prosperity or by a war with Japan. Al is, first of all, the only Democrat who can block the nomination of Franklin Roosevelt. Smith's statement—dog in the manger as many Roosevelt men regard it—is the first real check to the Roosevelt boom. Smith is solid with the Raskob gang which controls the Democratic

National Organization and which holds the party mortgages. The Raskobites don't like Roosevelt, never have and never will. They regard him as an outsider, too independent, a sort of kibitzer at the great game of politics. Smith may not finally get the nomination but he can at least split Roosevelt's New York support, simply by being "available"; he can divide Roosevelt's strength in the wet East and he can force the selection of a candidate who will sign on the dotted line and do right by our Nell. There is no gratitude in politics. Roosevelt put Smith's name in nomination in 1924 and 1928 and ran for Governor in 1928 at Smith's urgent request. Smith was defeated; Roosevelt was elected and re-elected. Smith didn't quite like it. Last year he opposed Roosevelt's policy on reforestation, only to have the New York voters agree overwhelmingly with Roosevelt. The appearance of his "might choose to run" statement has caused his name to be entered for the primaries in several States where Roosevelt had a chance to overcome the Raskob opposition. After all, it's only natural. Here, in 1932, is the big chance for a Democratic President to be elected and why should it not be Al Smith?

The answer to all charges of ingratitude is: "Boloney!" Smith has a perfect right to desire the nomination and the Presidency, and his friends have a perfect right to work for his success. Talk of a deep-dyed plot to block Roosevelt and clear the track for some fellow who will stand when hitched, a Jack Garner of Texas or a Governor Ritchie of Maryland, is so much moonshine. If Al wants the nomination, he wants it for himself, and not to spite Roosevelt, and the people of this country may as well get used to the idea that Smith is a real candidate and a pretty strong one, too.

With the dice loaded against him, he polled more votes than any Democratic candidate had ever received, and almost as many as were cast for Harding and Coolidge. The shift of 500,000 ballots would have given him the election of 1928. Now, with the Republican "Prosperity" argument knocked higher than a kite, with President Hoover's weird record of ungainly problems, stalled policies and rotten bad luck, with the wet sentiment rising and prices falling, Al Smith would make a very dangerous opponent for any Republican candidate. His greatest handicap, on form, would be that he was defeated once before and it is always easier to lick a man the second time.

As a politician, Al Smith has few equals. When one considers how completely the previous Democratic contenders have passed out of the picture, Al's "availability" is a miracle. Jimmy Cox, John Davis, William McAdoo —where are they now? On the sidelines or in the cheering section. But Al Smith has the knack of keeping himself in cold storage and still remaining a "hot tip" for the Presidential sweepstakes. As President, this political skill would be invaluable, since the Chief Executive must be a politician as well as a statesman and all the great Presi-

dental mistakes of the past twenty years simply empha-
size the fact that it is not a bad idea to put a good politician in the White House. At Albany, Smith mastered the
trick of teaching a Republican legislature the words to
his Democratic music. Smith in the White House would
get on better with Congress than any President since
Warren Gamaliel Harding.

It is rather difficult to see Smith as a national statesman. Does he know anything about national or international politics? Nobody seems to know, though everybody seems to feel that he would be flexible enough to
take advice and sensible enough to select good advisers.
In a period which may demand quick decisions and good
team work, rather than great brain work and careful
blueprinting, Al Smith's ability to work with men and
things as he finds them would be worth having in the
Presidency.

His past is an open book. He worked his way up from
the slums of New York's East Side to national prominence. From the Fulton Fish Market to the Governor's
Mansion at Albany and to the Democratic nomination
of 1928, he has marched with the help of Tammany
Hall. Yet no one has ever pinned a dirty dollar on him
or has fastened the taint of Tammany corruption upon
his political activity. He is a great vote-getter. He gave
the State of New York an efficient and enlightened administration, and much of Governor Roosevelt's reputation for sane progressivism is due to his pursuit of Smith

policies. Smith regularly made mincemeat of the Republican candidates for Governor and when he ran for the Presidency he staged a campaign which, for color and vigor, had not been equalled in this country since the days of Bryan. He accepted defeat like a man and built the Empire State Building while Hoover was discovering that the Presidency was a gold brick. Smith has brains, frankness, charm; he can get votes; and he is the luckiest man in America. If he had been elected just before the panic of 1929, no words would have been too black for him and he would have been condemned to oblivion and his party to complete collapse. As it is, when a politician has the reputation for ability, popularity *and* luck, he is sitting pretty.

So far as the issues of this election are concerned, Al Smith stands in the open on two of the three great principles which will arouse the voters. On Prohibition, he is a frank and personal wet, who drinks himself, who believes in States' Rights and would favor home rule on the liquor question. Raskob's recent questionnaire on Prohibition Repeal and his work for a Home Rule Amendment to the Prohibition law is squarely in line with Smith's views. So far as unemployment is concerned, Smith is for the Dole. At the Jackson Day Dinner last January, he came out bluntly and stated that the Federal Government would have to relieve the distress of the unemployed or a very dangerous situation would develop. On the issue of America First!—the new wave

32

of nationalism which swamped Hoover's war debt policy and made Newton Baker drop the League of Nations as an editor drops a war story in favor of the Lindbergh kidnaping—Al is not committed. He probably doesn't know or care two hoots about abroad, but, as a New Yorker, he would be inclined to take the say-so of the big bankers who played duck on a rock with our money in the foreign bond market. On the other hand, his interests have been so exclusively American that he has never been stamped as an internationalist and he could roar for isolation as loudly and sincerely as any other candidate.

He is a little shaky on minor issues: On the Tariff, he would favor reduction in a general sort of way. His water-power policy represents a sensible compromise between the ideal of public ownership and the fact of private operation. So far as Farm Relief is concerned, he probably thinks that the farmers have been getting a tough break but doesn't worry about it. On the issue of hard times, he knows—as only a man who has lived in the slums can know—what depression and unemployment mean to the self-respecting poor.

Everything that has happened since 1928 has played into his hands. As the wave of nationalism injures Baker and Roosevelt, Smith is untouched. As the breakdown of international finance discredits the Democratic international banking candidates—Owen D. Young and Melvin Traylor—Smith is unshaken. As hard times and un-

33

employment shake the confidence of the country in Hoover, Smith is an ideal candidate for the people who are suffering. As the wet tide rises, Smith's policy on Prohibition is becoming closer and closer to practical politics.

Smith's weakness—and it is so serious that he is regarded by many Democrats and some Republicans as the only man who can re-elect Herbert Hoover—lies in the character of his friends and of his foes. The lineup and prejudices of the election of 1928—the first Presidential campaign in this country to be fought and won on a religious issue—still stand. That campaign smashed the Solid South and developed hatreds and prejudices which have barely healed. Smith's renomination would be the signal for the reappearance of the passions which defeated him in 1928, and in their most dangerous form. If we had a bigotry when we were smug and prosperous, what would happen when we are poor and discontented?

Smith would be supported by the same big bankers and big industrialists who want a lower tariff, by the same liberals and progressives who are looking for something less like a bump on a logarithm in the White House, by the New York and Chicago political machines, by the aliens and new-stock Americans, by the Wets, by the cities, by the unemployed, by the East and North. He would be opposed by the Dries, the farmers, the Native Americans; by the reactionary politicians of the South, by the boosters of the West, and by the run of

34

the Chambers of Commerce and house-broken Labor Unions. Another 1928 campaign, conducted in time of depression, would shake this country to its foundations. His nomination four years ago cost the country a wave of bigotry and prejudice in both parties and in all sections, which practically paralyzed the power of the Government to deal intelligently with the liquor question and broke its will to ignore the commands of the political preachers and religious lobbies in the more vital matters of national defense. Another such campaign might easily take the form of a revolution in all but name.

If Al Smith were elected in 1932, it would symbolize a radical political upheaval in the United States. It would end the "country club" notion of citizenship, in which the children of recent immigrants are treated as second-class members not entitled to the full privileges of the club house. When the product of the slums and the beneficiary of a machine like Tammany can reach the White House, as well as reach for it, the long reign of the native American farmers—suspicious of the city feller—will have come to an end.

In office, Al Smith would not be committed, as Hoover is committed, to maintain any special policies. He would be liable to recommend unemployment insurance and to urge the modification of the Eighteenth Amendment; he would probably take the say-so of the international bankers that our tariff is too high; he could do little or nothing for the farmer and in the whole field of economic statesmanship he would tend to follow the Hoover policies.

What he would do in foreign affairs would, of course, be determined by events outside of his control. His affiliations would not dispose him to recognize Russia, but if Russian recognition becomes, as it may well become, the necessary step in the development of American policy in Manchuria, he would take his advice from his Secretary of State. He would tend, as any Democrat would tend, to strengthen our navy and to follow a less timid and petulant course in dealing with foreign powers. And he would select a good Cabinet and accept good advice, rather than try to make the Presidency a one-man show.

As matters stand, his chances of getting the Democratic nomination are only fair, although his chances of dictating the nomination are excellent. He can make Roosevelt the nominee and he can break Roosevelt. Yet his own candidacy is on a firmer basis than the bare facts of politics would indicate. Time has worked for Smith to discredit the Hoover Administration; time is now working for him, in the form of nationalism, to injure Roosevelt, Young and Baker, all of whom are tarred with internationalism, leaving Smith, the leader of his party, to face a field of "favorite sons" like Ritchie of Maryland, "dark horses" and "compromise candidates." His chances of winning the election are not so good, for his nomination would threaten another break in the Democratic Party and another campaign of hatred.

By the same token, Smith's chances, if elected, of going down to history as a major American statesman are very great indeed, for his success would be, in itself, as dramatic and significant as the election of Andrew Jackson in 1828 and of Abraham Lincoln in 1860. It would mark a social and political revolution in the United States and would signalize a new age of politics in the interest of the big cities, of the masses which inhabit them, and of the bankers which control them, rather than in the interest of the farmers, the countryside which they cultivate and the industrialists who direct their votes. Moreover, the events of 1933-37 are bound to be of such importance that whoever is head of the American Government at this time will be faced with the necessity for quick-witted and vigorous leadership. Al Smith has plenty of brains under his brown derby and plenty of guts. He is a man who thinks on his feet, fights hard and cleanly, and does not think he knows everything.

If, as seems quite possible, his candidacy causes a big fight in the Democratic camp and heartfelt rejoicing among the Republicans, and if he has the courage and the self-sacrifice to hold back the men who want him to make a Glory Hallelujah pre-convention campaign, it is not because he has lost his nerve. If he puts his candidacy into first gear now, when everything is coming his way, it is because he is too patriotic to subject his party or his country to another orgy of sectional hatred, or because he honestly doubts, as well he may, that he has the necessary economic and international background to lead the American nation during an era of economic turmoil and international unrest. Many of us feel that Al Smith will be too big a man to seek vindication at the polls in 1932 if he believes that the East Side slums, Tammany Hall, Albany and the Empire State Building are not enough of a political education for the statesman who must solve the currency problems, reorganize American agriculture, deal with the war debts, handle Manchuria, parry the thrusts of European diplomacy and brave the perils of international ill will in the second great political crisis of the twentieth century.

IV

Republican Runners-Up

A BOUT every twenty years we become terribly tired of the Republican Party. Sometimes we are merely bored and give them a warning and another chance; sometimes we vote them out of office; and sometimes the party gets so tired of itself that it splits. It takes about a generation to disgust people so thoroughly that they do something about the Republicans. In 1872, the disgust led to the creation of the Liberal Republican Party, which got exactly nowhere and did not prevent the re-election of General Grant. In 1892, we took the drastic step of electing a Democratic President. In 1912, the Progressives under Roosevelt split the party like a stick of kindling and let in Woodrow Wilson. What will happen in 1932?

One thing which will happen is a violent struggle for the future ownership of the party. Hoover has the nomination, if he wants it, and—as Cautious Cal is quoted— "Ef he don't want it, it wun't be wuth hevin'." Under the circumstances, you would expect the average politician to refuse to touch the Presidential beehive with a ten-foot pole and to regard the prospective candidate

39

with the mournful affection due a sacrificial goat. Already, you see the Vice Presidency being tossed around like a hot penny by an organ-grinder's monkey. Charley Curtis, the present occupant of the Vice-Presidential Black Maria, thought for a while of giving up his job and going back to the Senate where he will be safe for six years. Theodore Roosevelt, Jr., flirted with the office—was not the great T.R. Vice President once?—and Hanford MacNider, former chief of the American Legion and present Minister to Canada, was also mentioned as a possible victim. A post which is usually a gentle form of political euthanasia is becoming all but sacrificial. So far as the Republican Convention is concerned, one of the liveliest fights of 1932 will be the struggle by various astute politicians to avoid being given the short end of the nominations.

How does it happen that there is no struggle to avoid the admittedly hopeless contest with Hoover for the Presidential hole in the ticket? How does it happen that the "Draft Coolidge" talk hasn't been killed even by Cal's downright refusal to consider himself a party draught horse? How was it that the late Dwight Morrow was repeatedly and against his will named for the Presidency? How is it that the Hearst press and some unknown Ohio backers are starting an obviously futile campaign to make Senator Borah the Republican candidate? How is it that the Hiram Johnsons, the Brookharts and the Pinchots are running about emitting shrill squeals that anybody but Hoover must be chosen or all is lost?

The answer is that, in times of trouble, the party splits into two groups, and that these two groups fight to determine whether the old stand-pat conservative steam-roller crowd shall run the party or whether the Progressive and populistic crowd shall get control. It is a fight between East and West, between the bankers and business men with their long purses and their short memories, on the one hand, and the farmers, workers, debtors and voters, with their mortgages, their wage-cuts and their panaceas, on the other. Presidential boomlets are simply window-dressing designed to conceal the bitter battle for the platform—which is to say the principles—and the organization—which is to say the future control—of the larger American party.

So it happens that the convention will meet under an absolute necessity of renominating Hoover and will, at the same time, produce a lot of hopelessly out-distanced runners-up for the nomination, who will represent the real struggle between the Conservatives and the Progressives for the party's future, win or lose.

Hoover, like every Republican President, has to unite these two wings and, with them, all the issues which divide them. In times of prosperity, as under Coolidge, this doesn't matter; in times of depression, as at present, there is always the danger that the two wings will diverge so far as to split the Party or, what is even more painful, will rush together in a rage and crush the President.

Incredible as it may seem, the conservative Republicans—the Grundybund of tariff grabbers, the bankers who have been loaning our money abroad with both hands open and both eyes shut, the public utilities and railroad crowd, and the boys who contribute to the campaign funds—are very much concerned over Hoover's "radicalism." "Dammit, the man's a Socialist!" is the secret thought of the gouty lads in the club windows, who get calloused thumbs from clipping coupons and housemaid's knee from bending over safe-deposit boxes. His farm relief program, his Farm Board with its price-pegging and its competition with private speculators, his banking pool, his plan for pooling railway revenues, his projects for financing home construction through the land banks, all this is so close to Bolshevism for the old fellows who still privately consider the income tax as unconstitutional, that the wonder is they have not kicked him out before this.

Their resentment is the only logic back of the pathetic hope that somehow, somewhere, Calvin Coolidge may miraculously return to lead his people back to the long-green pastures. Poor, brilliant, self-effacing Dwight Morrow was their next best bet. Against his will, he was being groomed for the Presidency in the Wall Street district so gleefully that it was almost indecent. And the joke of it was that had Morrow lived, he would have scourged our panhandling financiers with scorpions, where Hoover simply makes them stay in after school. A recently reformed banker could have done things to Wall Street that never would have entered the honest old head of a retired engineer. With Morrow dead and Coolidge playing safe, the conservative Republicans lack what is known to football as a triple-threat man—one who can run, kick and pass the buck—and they will be gravely hampered in their struggle to keep the party safe for the moneybags and the forced-draught financiering which vanished like Nineveh when the stock market boiled over in 1929.

This leaves Hoover almost alone to face the onslaught of the Progressives in the fight for the platform. Only poor old Senator Fess of Ohio, who thinks that every Republican President is Jehovah's hired man, and a scattering of party wheel-horses, are left to defend Hoover from all sorts of malicious and felonious assaults, delivered, as is conventional, under a flag of truce. Mayhem is the least that some of those sons of the wild jackass will do to his political principles if they catch him out alone after dark.

Hence the loud blowing of horns and beating of drums in the alfalfa belt. The Progressives look upon the convention as the Assyrians looked on Babylon, the Japanese on Manchuria, and Blücher on London: "What a place to loot!" For twenty years, ever since Teddy Roosevelt campaigned to the characteristically modest strains of "Onward, Christian Soldiers," it has been pretty hard lines for the Progressives. Some have died, some have gone conservative and stout, all have grown old and grey and a little tottery, and a few, like La Follette in 1924 and Norris in 1928, have been able to stand it no longer and have burst through the party lines like a poodle jumping through a paper hoop. In the spring of 1932, they will have had a session of Congress in which they controlled the balance of power in the Senate and could make the difference between a deadlocked or a Democratic House of Representatives, and they are determined to shape the Republican platform and to inherit the Republican Party, with or without Hoover's consent.

This is rather hard on Hoover, for the Progressives despise him for his stand-pat conservatism as keenly as the conservatives hate him for his "radicalism." And so it happens that when you read the roster of the Progressive "candidates" for the nomination you have read a list of everything which the Progressives hope to read into a party which was once the only party for a free American. You will also have read a list of the bitter mouth-washes which Herbert Hoover may have to gargle in the course of the campaign.

Gifford Pinchot of Pennsylvania is too old a man and too old a hand at politics to dream that he, who once served with Roosevelt and quarreled with Taft, can beat Hoover to the post. What Pinchot wants is to rivet a bone-dry prohibition policy on the party, to commit it to the idea that the Federal Government must care for the unemployed, and to curb the autocracy of the public utility barons who play hopscotch with the Federal Power Commission and the Interstate Commerce Act. Senator Borah, bell-voiced, beetle-browed, bull-necked playboy of the Senate, is far too wise to trade his post as Chairman of the Foreign Relations Committee and critical spokesman-at-large for the hazards and compromises and worries of responsible administration. His clandestine "availability" means that he, who has become a symbol of political liberalism, intends to fight for progressive campaign policies. Charley Curtis of Kansas, with his ponderous cogitations, his geniality and his prairie shrewdness, represents the Mid-Western farmer and the latter's artless belief that it is up to Washington to make wheat-growing profitable. Of them all, Hiram Johnson of California, the bitterest Hoover-hater in the party, the man who could have been President if he had accepted the offer of the Vice Presidency in 1920 and who would have made a great President, is the only one whose principles are of the old rugged American school of Rooseveltian power and push. Between them, the Progressive leaders represent nationalism of the Big Stick variety, isolation of the pre-Wilsonian brand, prohibition of the pre-Volstead vintage, and social progress of the late Victorian kind. Between them they could play the

Republican Party like an accordion but could they make the American nation dance to its tunes?

To oppose these shock troops, Hoover can mobilize little but the party hacks—the Senator Watsons, Smoots, Moseses, Shortridges and such—who, under the mask of party loyalty, are seething with resentment at what they call Hoover's "flabbiness." By this they mean Hoover's failure to keep the country safe for Republican office-holders. The hacks will do their duty like any other set of strike breakers and will obey orders, but they will not waste many tears if the Hoover steam roller gets stalled in one or another of the little last-ditch trenches which will scar the Republican convention.

The convention will contain as many side-shows as a three-ring circus and should be almost as funny. There will be Senator Norris and his power issue, with its danger of frightening the big money into the Democratic coffers. There will be the battle to control the California delegation, between Hoover and Johnson, in order to decide whether Hoover is a "favorite son" or just an immigrant from Iowa. Hence the Administration's policy in Manchuria, as well as being sound American policy, is good politics in California, with its anti-Japanese sentiment. Then there will be the orphaned wets, with no one to lead them now that Senator Morrow has gone, and with nowhere to go except into the dry camp, bag and baggage. Then there will be the shake-down gang on the side-lines: the tariff fixers, the professional veterans with itching palms, the farmers with that tired feeling, the bankers who play for tax and currency favors, the anti-Europeans having convulsions in front of the World Court, the pro-Europeans led by Nicholas Murray Butler burning candles in front of the shrine of the League of Nations. Everybody will be fighting everybody else, and it will be anybody's war.

For the Republican platform of 1932 will be the battle of the century. Campaign pledges don't count for much but they must sound plausible. What will the party say about the tariff? Too high? Ouch! Too low? (Groans from manufacturers.) Just right? What! ! It's hard to make Smoot's masterpiece revive sufficiently to walk to the hospital, let alone lead a torch-light parade to the ballot box. They will probably say that some rates are too high, some too low, but that all can be adjusted in time and that anyhow the Democrats voted for it.

And what except "Oh! my God!" can the Republicans say about prosperity? That it would have been worse but for Hoover? That we are on the upgrade? That we *have* prosperity? That it's all the fault of the world depression? Probably they will say all of this and then add that, had the Democrats been in power, we would have been utterly destroyed.

These questions are child's play compared to the party's stand on unemployment, on foreign affairs, on prohibition, on water power, on taxation, on currency, on agriculture. Shall the government feed the unemployed

47

or shall it trust to luck to avoid revolutionary unrest? Shall America in effect join the League of Nations or shall we isolate ourselves and let the rest of the world go to hell in its own way, without the priceless benefit of our good advice? Shall we have another round of the Eighteenth Amendment or shall we let the drinks go down the red lane? Shall the government go into the power business or shall it build very expensive dams for the benefit of private interests? Shall we rob the rich to help the poor or tax everybody impartially to serve the State? Shall we debase our money in order to produce an imitation of high prices or shall we stick to gold and pay the high price for low prices? Shall we pay the farmer to run his business at a loss or leave him to the mercy of the mortgage sharks? And that only starts the trouble, as every fight fits into and reinforces every other fight. Shall we subsidize the farmer if the farmer won't let us drink? Shall we refrain from taxing the rich if we don't feed the hungry? Shall we do anything at all or shall we simply turn the whole mess over to the Democrats?

That is the meaning of all these Republican Presidential "possibilities" when even a Congressman can see that Hoover is the only man who has a Chinaman's chance. That is what makes the Republican convention of 1932 in some ways more important than the election. Elections come and go, but parties keep on running, year in and year out. It may make very little real difference to the country as a whole whether Hoover or Roosevelt is elected. It will make a tremendous difference if the Republican Party, after sixty years of almost reactionary control, suddenly becomes the property of a group of aged radicals, whose "progressive ideas" are the product of the tin-pot social struggles of twenty and thirty years ago and whose most radical venture would be an attempt to impose the ideas of 1910 on the country instead of the ideas of 1890.

There won't be a Republican split in 1932. The Progressives learned their lesson in 1912 when the Roosevelt-Taft quarrel put the party in the control of the reactionaries and for twenty years left the Progressives on the inside looking out, like any convicted wife-beater. There may be a Republican victory as in 1872 or a defeat as in 1892, but the Republicans can survive a defeat. They would come back in 1936 or 1940. What the runners-up for Hoover's renomination want to determine is that, when the Republicans do come back, it will be as a party in which the common American can feel at home. Unfortunately for the Progressives, their particular brand of "common American" has been dead for twenty years.

The best tip on the election is to watch the Republican platform and the Democratic candidate. Between them lies the secret of this country's future. It looks bad either way.

V

The Democratic Field

ONCE in a lifetime the Democratic Party has a chance to win the Presidency. Between times the Democrats go through the motions of electioneering: they solemnly select a nominee who hypnotizes himself into believing that he will be elected; they adopt—after prolonged squabbles—an interesting and intricate party platform; and on election day it's all washed out and the Democratic candidate retires, full of honors and of prunes, to await the next sucker. So it was in 1896, 1900, 1904 and 1908, when Bryan ran three times out of four; so it was with Jimmy Cox in 1920, so with John W. Davis in 1924, and so with Al Smith in 1928. Will it be so in 1932?

The answer lies in whether the Democrats decide to follow a leader or an idea. Whenever they get an idea, the Democrats are licked. They have guessed wrong on every major political issue since and including the Civil War —they were wrong about Reconstruction, on the low tariff, on Free Silver, on anti-imperialism, on the League of Nations and on Prohibition. Their ideas may have been eternally right in theory, but they were wrong in

fact at the ballot box. Only two Democrats have occu-
pied the White House in the last seventy years. Each of
these men happened to be a leader and was bigger than
his party, in the first case, and bigger than his country, in
the second case. Grover Cleveland stood for uncompro-
mising honesty in public life—he was not a clever man,
but he *was* a fighter. Woodrow Wilson stood for uncom-
promising intelligence in public life—he was not a good
party leader or even a nationalist, but *he* was a fighter.
Both men won the nomination against stubborn opposition and carried the country because the American people like fighters and prefer a fight to coolly scientific
statesmanship or to honest party leadership.

On that account, we don't worry much about the
platform or the principles of our minority party, except
as a sort of political scarecrow. We know perfectly well
that the Democrats can't control Washington long
enough to execute a radically new national policy. So it
happens that the Democratic platform fight will be a
side show, designed at most to enable the party leaders
to remain in good humor. Win or lose, the Democratic
Party won't need a platform in 1932. Their experience
in 1928 has convinced them that people vote *against* one
candidate rather than *for* his opponent. For the Democrats, the platform will consist of two words: "Herbert
Hoover." The paramount issue on which they will appeal
to the country is: "Herbert Hoover." And the only na-

tional policy which they can offer with any hope of accomplishment is: "Down with Herbert Hoover!"

Such a policy, with its eager and innocent capitalization of all the accumulated discontent of three years of hard times, calls for a fighter who can dramatize it. Hence the squabble about the platform will amount to little: the real battle will be for the nomination. For the first time in a generation the Democrats have a chance to capture the White House and you won't see them handing the nomination to anyone on a silver platter.

Roosevelt is in the lead, Roosevelt is the favorite in the betting and in the nation-wide polls, but a bare one-third of the delegates will suffice to block his nomination and the conservative Democratic bloc is scurrying to tie up those votes and to stop him at almost any price.

This is not the rule-or-ruin, dog-in-a-manger policy which it appears to be. If the Democratic High Command is correct in betting that, other things being equal, any fighting Democrat can beat Hoover, they are wise to fight shy of Roosevelt. Roosevelt, or any other Liberal Democrat, can expose his party to defeat simply by being a liberal. The world is staging a big swing away from radicalism and towards conservative nationalism, even in Soviet Russia. The huge victory of the Conservatives in England on a patriotic program, the capture of the Japanese Government by the militarist party, the dominance of Hitlerism in Germany, the persistence of Mussolini, the stiffening of national lines and the eclipse of internationalism and of socialism throughout the Western nations, mean that the Democrats are in danger, if they run a liberal. An unscrupulous Republican campaign could pin the red label on any liberal opponent and could resort to patriotism—the last refuge of the politician—as a winning issue for Hoover.

The safe and sane wing of the party would like to copper its bets and anticipate the dreadful tactics which crumpled up the British Labour Party like a sheet of wet blotting paper. Their weakness is that they have no real candidate to offer. Owen D. Young, who was the Democratic bondholder's hope a couple of years ago, the peripatetic "world citizen" of the General Electric Company and the supreme recipient of honorary degrees, is now under a double cloud. He represents the internationalism of the biggest sort of Big Business, to which interest rates are more important than boundaries, and collateral than patriotism, of super-national finance with its unanswerable list of defaulted securities and depreciated currencies and once-bitten-twice-shy American investors. Internationalism and big business are not what they used to be when the New York *Times* had editorial hiccoughs every time Mr. Young emitted a baccalaureate address at some mid-western college. In the second place, Owen Young's great achievement was the Young Plan which "finally solved" the German reparations question in 1929, just about the time that our Stock Market was ready to have economic kittens in Morgan's front parlor.

The Young Plan today looks as though it had suffered "a fate worse than death" down one or another of the dark alleys of world diplomacy, and the reparations question is again squalling on our door-step.

So the right wing of the party, headed by Barney Baruch, has quietly begun to rally the coupon-cutters behind that Adonis of Annapolis, Governor Ritchie of the Free State of Maryland. Ritchie is the handsomest man in his state. He is a states'-rights wet and he has been wet since the day when Volstead was a Congressman and not a memory. He is "right" on public utilities and on the ideal of keeping the government out of business. He is near enough to the South to rank as a southerner and close enough to the North to claim northern support. He is an able executive, a shrewd, attractive and skilful politician. He is as good a stalking-horse or dark horse as ever went into a convention with the prestige of a "favorite son" and the availability of a "compromise candidate." The chief barrier to his nomination is his dripping-wet attitude.

For the traditional party-battle over prohibition will not carry any candidate very far. Both sides are worn out. Al Smith is the logical choice of the wringing-wet crowd and he will remain in the field, both as a possibility and a threat, until the drys promise to behave themselves until election day. Faint murmurs from the drys insist that William Gibbs McAdoo, Wilson's able Secretary of the Treasury, who fought Smith to a standstill in 1924, has one more fight left in him, but McAdoo is too big a man to waste himself or his energies on a play designed merely to put a detour sign on the Sidewalks of New York. The Smith crowd still don't quite realize that their day is over and Al himself would like another chance, but he can't make the grade. At most he could split the New York delegation and weaken Roosevelt, but there's no percentage in that for a man of Smith's caliber.

The real rival to Roosevelt on the liberal side is the man who may become either the convention's compromise or its Vice-Presidential candidate: Newton D. Baker of Ohio. Ohio is a pivotal state and Baker is the rarest of American politicians—an individualist. A pacifist, he was one of our great Secretaries of War. An idealist and a reformer, he has an expert grasp of practical executive detail. A gentleman and a scholar, he is not panting after the nomination even as the hart panteth after the water-brooks. He does not conform. He favors modification of the prohibition law and American entry into the League of Nations. Shy, sensitive, unassuming, he is—in his own way—a sort of Democratic Dwight Morrow. Should the conservatives block Roosevelt, Baker stands a more than excellent chance of emerging from the convention as the Democratic candidate, and he would make a good candidate and a first-rate President.

However, at the present time, the Democratic foreground is cluttered up with "favorite sons," the old device of local candidacies by which a promising national candidacy can be headed off. Between them, they may pile up enough delegates to stop Roosevelt short of the necessary two-thirds majority. Jim Ham Lewis, dripping-wet senator from Illinois, who defeated Ruth Hanna McCormick, may well carry that pivotal state's delegation into the convention behind him in support of the favorite son of New Jersey, Governor Harry Moore. Jim Reed of Missouri, the bitter and scorpion-tongued foe of internationalism, the senator who raised national isolation to a religion and helped wreck the Treaty of Versailles, is angling for the Missouri delegation. Senator Bulkley and Governor White of Ohio, both Democrats, the first wet and the second dry, will control the delegation from another key-state. Senator Swanson of Virginia is actively supporting the candidacy of ex-Governor Harry Byrd, brother of the ubiquitous explorer without whose presence no Pole need consider itself on the map. Senator Joe Robinson of Arkansas, Smith's running-mate in 1928 and Democratic leader in the Senate, is another favorite son with strong backing in the Democratic Southwest. Cockleburr Bill Murray, Governor of Oklahoma, is being put forward as a Jacksonian populist and will receive strong backing from the poor-white, hill-billy, down-and-out, under-dog element which undermines the political pretensions of the stately orators of the Solid South. His candidacy is not to be despised in a region which has elected Huey Long Senator from Louisiana and Bilbo Governor of Mississippi.

All of these favorite sons are able politicians and would make fighting candidates. Not one of them packs a winning punch, but as the national election may be decided on form, if the Democrats guess right, that doesn't bother them much at this stage of the game.

The real meaning of this multiplication of candidates is that it indicates the inevitable and historic split in the party. If the split can be kept in the background until after election day, well and good. If it develops at the convention, as in 1924, it may wreck the party. If it develops during the campaign, as in 1928, it may lose the election. It is a serious matter and goes to the very roots of our political system.

For convenience, the two wings of the party may be described as the Raskob gang and the Methodist gang. John J. Raskob, angel of the party's finances, wet, Catholic, big-business, friend of Al Smith, knows his way around New York City. He senses the uneasiness near the altars of high finance, the whiff of drainage in the odor of financial sanctity, and is worried lest the Democratic Party get above itself and vote for an "impossible" candidate. The big boys are quite willing to let the Democrats rouse the rabble on the issue of prohibition to a "Down with Hoover" battle-cry, just as in 1920 they let the Republicans fight on the issue of the League of Nations to the tune of "Down with Wilson." They emphatically do not want the election to degenerate into a line-up of the rich against the poor, on the issue of hard times and how to end them.

On the other hand, the Methodist gang represents the simple and melodeon-minded American population of the rural South and Southwest, with its prejudices against liquor and "furriners," but also with its distrust of bankers, of Wall Street and of the East in general. The Methodists ought to be sidetracked from considering why they are expected to pay their mortgages while war debts must be canceled, onto the perfectly harmless topic of prohibition. At the moment, however, it looks as though any man who promised in ringing terms to lead the Methodists against the money-changers, publicans and sinners of Lower Manhattan, and against their allies in the conservative South, would meet with enthusiastic support such as that given to Bryan when he promised cheap money and the easy repayment of debt in 1896. It cost big money to stop Bryan in the national election and it would cost millions to stop another Bryan in 1932. It would be cheaper to spend a little to keep him from being nominated at all.

That is why the Democratic convention is anybody's fight. The only question is whether the Democrats will save their fighting for the Republicans and iron out their difficulties in order to present a united front. Probably not. The tradition of the "damn-fool Democrats" dies hard. Even in 1912, Woodrow Wilson had a terrific battle against Champ Clark, who entered the convention as favorite and was beaten only because Bryan, then leader of the Methodist gang, drove August Belmont and the Wall Street Democrats out of the convention and then threw all his support to Wilson. A united Democratic Party won that election (under a fighter), only because the Republicans were split. On how the Democrats handle the same problem in 1932, with the Republicans united, depends the question of whether Big Business will actually switch its financial support from the majority to the minority party.

For Big Business likes to come in on the winning side, especially if the winner is a radical. There's no profit in backing a loser unless you have backed the winner far more heavily. Business backs both parties and all important candidates as a matter of business, and so is in a position to ask favors, heads or tails. If a fighting Democrat, like Bryan or Wilson, sweeps the convention and embarks upon a vigorous liberal campaign, money may be scared into the Republican camp. Business won't like that, and the Democratic Party won't like it either, and if the Democrats win, Big Business will have a hard four years. On the other hand, if the Democratic Party puts up a nice, safe and sane, colorless candidate, many discontented voters will decide to stick to Hoover or to vote Socialist, and the party will have lost the chance of a lifetime.

Pity the poor Democrats! They have to choose between a man of courage who will dare to risk the party fortunes in a bold fight for national power and a man who will try to please Mr. Raskob's big-bottomed, blue-jowled coupon-clippers at the risk of losing the election. The best bet is that the Democrats will choose a fighter. They are a pugnacious lot and have never refused a battle which they had a fair chance of winning.

VI

Hungry Democrats

To THE average American the activities of the two
political parties are about as edifying as a cross-
section of a mad-house; their antics are conducted with
the dreadful solemnity of violent paranoia but their significance in terms of day-to-day living is practically nil.
They are regarded as part of the national show, alongside
of the annual selection of "Miss America" and the tub-
thumping of evangelists and Rotarians.

Nevertheless, the political parties are now a definite
instrument of the American Government and their re-
spective national committees and conventions are far
more important than many of the better-advertised
clauses of the Constitution, for all that they have no
standing in that sacred document. They are the practical
means by which a successful candidate and group of
politicians rule the country. In fact, without parties it
would be next to impossible to administer the United
States; Presidents would be powerless to secure co-operation from Congress and Congress would be unable to
pursue a coherent and respectable legislative policy.

The force which has created our political parties is—

speaking brutally—the lure of government jobs. If the President did not have the power to appoint or nominate the office-holders, the political machinery would lack motive power. Differences of opinion would spring up in Congress and would coagulate into little local or sectional groups; adventurous cliques and cabals would form; legislation would be open to direct bribery, coercion or demagoguery, and American government would be more of a mess than it is. Admittedly, possession of the public payroll is the beginning and the end of party organization in the United States. Patronage is a bribe or a club with which to disarm opposition or compel support; without the jobs a President can get nowhere; with them, he can count on party discipline and party support.

Working from the basis of the public payroll, as the first object of political action, getting elected becomes the means. This is expensive and demands a party program by which campaign funds can be collected from the beneficiaries of such action as the party proposes to take, and the voter can be aroused to support the Party rather than the Man as a means of expressing his ideas. The Republicans have pre-empted most of those appeals to the pocketbook which are calculated to yield political dividends—the tariff, tax reduction, oil and power resources, protection of property and non-interference with profits—and hence they have largely monopolized the jobs and the Presidency, leaving the Democrats a minority party and with few visible means of support.

As a result, the Democrats are not a disciplined or coherent political group, they have not had an opportunity
to train or advertise their leaders at public expense, and,
on the basis of efficiency, are not a reliable means of
achieving any national policy. Being the weaker group,
they must continually take the offensive and, being on
the outside looking in, they can never be sure that their
opposition will not weaken and divide their own forces
still further or that the Republicans will not steal the
more appealing portions of their platform. Under those
circumstances, only a first-rate national calamity offers
them a chance of obtaining power or of keeping it once
they have secured it.

Such is the regular set-up. In 1932, all that is changed
and we see the astounding sight of a minority party
going into a critical election without any real policy,
relying upon the vote of protest against hard times to
sweep them into office. Playing politics with human mis-
ery thus becomes their soundest policy. The one thing
which would utterly destroy their chances of victory
would be the return of visible prosperity before election
day. Accordingly, the one thing they really dread is the
swift reduction of unemployment and the rapid rise of
prices. As they are the party which benefits from hard
times, good times would cook their goose. This year
it looks as though they were right in believing that
Hoover won't get the boys out of the breadlines by

Christmas, so they feel free to adopt the most daringly original attitude ever assumed by a weaker party against a discredited and distracted majority: an attitude of cynical inaction.

This means that the only real Democratic issue in this election is, "Turn the rascals out!" It is unnecessary for them to add the corollary to this slogan: "Give us their jobs!" For things equal to the same thing are equal to each other and we can rest assured that the Democrats will feel no diffidence at taking over every public job from dog catcher up, if they can get the necessary power from the electorate.

This is common sense. The Democrats are hungry for public office. They are not callous towards the unemployed; they have been suffering the agonies of political unemployment ever since 1921. If they are unable to agree on anything else, they can all agree on the necessity for taking the jobs away from the Republicans and refreshing themselves at the Federal Treasury. It is elemental self-preservation which drives them—not partisan greed—and if they can get power they will make a clean sweep of every appointive office in the bestowal of the Presidency. They will man the ship with an inexperienced crew, officered by a few survivors from the Wilsonian era, and put to sea in the worst political gale in a century. Otherwise, how shall they reward their party leaders and train their future statesmen? How else can they restore their party morale and prevent their general disintegration? Even as the amœba, in subdividing, strives to preserve the race of amœbæ from extinction, so the Democrats, in rushing for the offices, are striving to preserve the Democratic Party.

Except for the hunger for public office, there is no common bond between the members of the party. The party itself is the prisoner of the Solid South and the South is the prisoner of the black man. The Negro problem is the backbone of the party, which thereby becomes a racial party and hence a sectional party. It extends from Southeast to Southwest, while the real divisions of economic interest run from North to South, and the real divisions of political opinion cannot be trapped by geographical boundaries. In this sense, the Democrats are a weak imitation of the heterogeneous Republicans, with the added element of demoralizing and paralyzing feuds, all of which, in the last analysis, are the result of the Negro problem and the Civil War.

The war between Catholics and Protestants is nowhere so bitter as within the party whose founder, Thomas Jefferson, was the author of religious toleration in the United States. Catholic vs. Methodist, wet vs. dry, city vs. country, the South vs. the North, the section vs. the Nation, low tariff vs. protection, debtor vs. creditor— all of these naked political manias rage unchecked in the party which has neither the power nor the offices to apply like lotions to the inflamed prejudices of the color-conscious Southerner. To keep the Negroes from getting gin, the South sacrifices the Democratic theory of States' Rights; to keep the Negroes from voting, the South sacrifices the Declaration of Independence; to keep the Negroes from realizing their economic and industrial power, the white men of the South set their faces against anything in the nature of union organization or industrial justice. To retain the South's control of the party, democratic forms are sacrificed and militant Northern leaders, such as Smith, are scrapped. There is no essential unity in the Democratic organization.

The party organization is itself suspicious and autocratic, being based more on the desire to preserve the Solid South than to effect popular rule. In the Democratic National Convention, by the "unit rule," an entire state delegation can be compelled to vote for the candidate who is supported by a majority of that delegation. This minority party suffers no petty minorities to have a voice in its final policy. At the same time, not a simple but a two-thirds majority of all the delegates must vote for a candidate before he can be nominated by the Convention. Thus the Solid South perpetuates a veto power over the entire party. In the southern states, the Republican Party is virtually an illegal organization; this means that the Democrats of the South serve term after term in Congress and, by virtue of the seniority rule, stand to head all congressional committees whenever the party is in power. And finally, through the

Democratic caucus, the northern Democrats in Congress can be compelled to toe the line by the southern Democrats.

The continuing agency of the party is the national committee, composed of a man and woman from each state, selected by the state organizations, under the chairmanship of the man selected by the party's national candidate. Thus Al Smith's choice—John J. Raskob—has run the official organization since 1928 and, by buying up the party's debts, has secured a financial half nelson on the organization. He is responsible for the establishment of a permanent Executive Committee at Washington, headed by Jouett Shouse, which, with the aid of an expert publicity man, Charley Michelson, has applied national advertising methods to the serious business of discrediting the Hoover administration. Michelson's "battle of the mimeographs," his timely, forceful, shrewd and biting comments, fed to the press by carefully selected Democratic spokesmen, forced the Republicans to parallel this system and to hire their own publicity expert—Jimmy West—to issue mimeographs in a counter-barrage. The result, measured by election returns, has been the overwhelming victory of Michelson; nevertheless, when it comes to compelling the party to back water on prohibition, not even Raskob's money and position can sway the southern grip on the black man's gin.

Nothing seems to avail against the real Democratic

curse. They have lost their inferiority complex and, after the astounding 1928 election, in which they secured six million more votes than ever before, they begin to hope for a shift of the northern and western masses to their banner. Nevertheless, the party as a whole has experienced a steady deterioration since 1860 and is now primarily a sectional organization with a few vigorous local allies in the North, chiefly machine politicians of the least attractive type and Northern rebels against the Republican machines. Only in the amazing Smith campaign were the Democrats able to command national support. One by one they have dropped the issues and ideas—States' Rights, low tariff, popular sovereignty—which gave them their sixty years of supremacy before the Civil War, and now they stand stripped of all pretensions to national leadership in any field of economic or social action: and this at a time when vigorous leadership is the country's greatest need.

By one of the most disturbing paradoxes of politics, it is precisely this fact that gives them a chance at the national administration, and if March 4, 1933, sees a Democrat taking the oath of office at the Capitol it may be because the party is incapable of doing anything but "laying low and saying nuffin' " at the time of national crisis. Hence one asks: "After the inauguration—what?"

Their record is not reassuring. Having had only two Presidents since the Civil War, they have had to take their support where they could find it, and the source of their support has seldom been truly national. Accordingly, their domestic policies have invariably led to dissatisfaction and confusion so serious that they have yielded to the temptation to distract the public by pursuing a vigorous or even a violent foreign policy. So it was with Cleveland and the Venezuela business; so with Wilson and Mexico. So it will be in the future. Again, favoring a low tariff in theory, if not in practice, they have the support of the "international bankers" who are interested in the flow of credit rather than in the protection of American industry. Hence the Democrats in office have to take their financial orders from the biggest bankers. It was Cleveland who called in the elder J. P. Morgan and submitted to his dictation in the gold crisis of the 'Nineties. And it was Wilson who used Liberty Loan funds to relieve J. P. Morgan & Co. from the menace of exhausted British credit in 1917. As international finance has, in the past, been largely British, it has followed that the Democratic Party—for all its Irish members—has been the pro-British party in the United States. At least it was so regarded by the British Minister in Cleveland's day and certainly the Wilson Cabinet, from 1914 to 1917, was individually and collectively so favorable to the British cause in the World War that they permitted the British to set up faintly camouflaged recruiting-offices in the United States, and when it looked as though Wilson were going to make a vigorous protest against British blockade measures, Walter Hines

Page, his ambassador at London, evaded orders to such effect that the reluctant effort to preserve our neutral rights miscarried.

Finally, the Democratic Party is not a liberal party, for all of its canonization of Thomas Jefferson. It was Cleveland who used the American army as strike breakers in the industrial battles of the 1880's and '90's. It was Wilson's Attorney-General who in 1919 began the series of Red scares and Red raids and who used the Espionage Act to crush political radicalism in the United States. In fact, the Democratic Party in office is peculiarly the party of liquid wealth, international finance and forced social conformity.

This on the record. What the party would do in office in 1933 is another matter. It can be taken for granted that its leaders would be true to their salt and would try to play the banker's game—cancel the war debts, lower the tariffs, and "reform the Reds with rope." It can be assumed that they would try to do something safe but spectacular in Latin America or in Eastern Asia to distract popular attention from what was happening at home. It can also be assumed that they would try to cultivate the easy approval of the idealists by joining the World Court and the League of Nations and playing the British game in Europe against the French and their allies.

It is doubtful, however, that the rank and file of the party would stand for much of this denationalized leadership. With every decade since the Civil War, the party has become more national-minded and has reached a stage where it now regards world politics from an American rather than a Confederate point of view. Hence there would be a chance that, rather than follow Democratic policy to its logical conclusions, the party would smash its leaders and go to pieces as it did in the closing years of the Wilson administration, thereby bringing back the Republicans.

For it is the Democratic fate to play into the hands of calamity. It took a near panic and a split in the Republican ranks to elect Wilson in 1912, a World War to re-elect him in 1916, while only the disintegration of the solar system could have saved the party in 1920. Now a world-wide economic catastrophe is giving the Democrats another chance. That might not be such a bad thing for the country. Under vigorous leadership they could change many of the outworn or inappropriate policies of the Republicans. The Republicans are wedded to those policies, even where they are sick of them, and they cannot consistently divorce them. A change of administration permits both a change of policy at Washington and a change of Republican measures. So a Democratic administration, with all of its shortcomings, might prove to be precisely what this country needs after twelve years of stuffy and congested government by old men in the name of obsolete ideas. We can rely upon the common sense and the patriotism of the

Democratic rank and file to save us from the worst follies of what big bankers think is practical politics. The Democrats might lift the country and the Republican Party out of their ruts and start us off on a new track. This would be cheap at the price of a new set of office-holders, and if the inevitable collision between the party and its leaders led to the final break-up of the Democratic Party, with its autocratic organization and its stupefying subservience to the nigger-conscious satrapies of the Solid South, it would be the greatest political reform of our generation. For the country needs two real political parties, and as long as the Democratic Party is a league to protect the South against the Negro, so long will our politics revolve in a deadly circle, combining the mechanical repetition of sheer idiocy with dangerous paroxysms of homicidal mania, according to the pattern which has been imposed upon the country for the last seventy years of Republican ascendancy and Democratic desire for office.

VII

Smug Republicans

THE Republicans have been in power so long that they take it for granted that they are the only party fit to govern. They no longer realize that nothing is more fragile than popular approval in a country which is easily bored with self-advertised virtue and in which the national slogan is "Try anything once." The Grand Old Party has been drifting and dreaming along the line of least resistance and greatest profit for generations, and not once in that time has it had to take the political offensive. Instead, it has won elections by mudslinging and has cleverly avoided anything in the nature of political ideas.

It has seen political movements come and go, parties form and vanish, and has come to the conclusion that it need do nothing about anything, except advocate prosperity, raise the tariff, relieve the farmer, curse the Democrats, and let nature take its course. It does not worry about its voting strength, being confident that, as the representative of American nationalism and economic production, it can always see the Democrats and raise them one in a country in which production is an obsession and nationalism an instinct. So when Bryan, in 1896, polled the largest Democratic vote in a generation, the Republicans edged him out by a 600,000 majority; so in 1928, when Al Smith doubled the normal Democratic vote, the Republicans topped his figure by six million ballots and gave Hoover the greatest electoral majority in American history. And in general, the Republican vote has kept pace with the growth of the nation, where the Democratic vote has only kept pace with the growth of the white population of the South.

This is the Republican secret: they are a national party. They are at their weakest in local and off-year elections; at their strongest in Presidential elections. They have gambled on the fundamental soundness of American civilization and on the natural increase of American wealth. Where the Democrats go chasing after some vague idea of the welfare of humanity—did not Wilson warn us that to reject the Treaty of Versailles would "break the heart of the world"?—and have yammered about world trade, the Republicans have catered to much lower instinct with "America first!" and Prosperity: the Full Dinner Pail, Two Cars in Every Garage, and so on. By this means, their party has grown into the strangest conglomeration of conflicting viewpoints, held together by crude material interests and by patriotic prejudices, that the world has ever seen. The Republicans include the Negroes whom they freed in the Civil War, the big and hard-boiled industrialists of the East and Middle West, the socialistic Progressives of Wisconsin and the prairie states, the wool and cattle ranchers of the Rocky Mountains, the miners, the wheat and corn farmers of the Mississippi Basin, the big railroads and public utilities, the Pacific lumber and fruit interests, the immigrant masses of most of the big cities west of New Jersey and north of Maryland, liberals and conservatives, protectionists and free traders, wets and drys, pro- and anti-Europeans, all held together in the communion of the pocket book and by the creed of "Don't Knock! Boost!"

The only menace to the solidity of this confederacy is the risk of an occasional depression which knocks the stuffing out of the pocket book and makes the boosters look ridiculous. In the long run, in gambling on American prosperity the Republicans are betting on a sure thing. With a vigorous and inventive people, vast natural resources, a pretty good climate and the most habitable portion of the world's richest continent to work with, the Republicans can always take credit for the sunshine and can capitalize the inevitable growth of our power and numbers. Adversity and depression smash this pretty picture. The panic of 1929 and the hard times of 1930, 1931 and 1932 have turned the Republican battle cries against the G.O.P. The party which has reduced the income tax four times since the war and has retired ten billions of the public debt—amid loud cheers —now finds itself faced with a rising debt and increased taxes. The pocket nerve is pained and the bond of mutual interest which has united the party in the past doesn't look any less depreciated than those other bonds which we were persuaded to buy in the days of our prosperity. Hence, for a long time the Republicans refused to admit that we were having a depression and now their only fear is that the world catastrophe cannot be visibly patched up before election day. For they are the victims of their own argument, that the country votes for prosperity and not for any particular party.

They go into action this year, weaker and more demoralized than at any time in a generation. They are pinned down to the defensive at their weakest point: the President. Herbert Hoover promised the country prosperity and look what happened! He promised to put agriculture on a parity with industry, loaned the farmers half a billion of our dollars, established the Farm Board, and wheat dropped to the lowest price recorded in our history. He offered us a constructive work-out of the noble experiment and then gave the Wickersham Report a kick in the teeth when it suggested modification of the Volstead Act. He promised skilled management of the public finances, only to give up a quarter of a billion dollars in annual income from the War Debts and to present the nation with the two largest peace-time deficits in our history. He fought unemployment relief and vainly vetoed the bonus grab at a time when the unemployed and the veterans were threatening to sell out to any party which made it worth their while, and he has consistently attacked socialism while putting into force one socialistic measure after another. For every one of these "mistakes," he and his party have a good alibi or a rational defense but they *are* mistakes from the political point of view. He has dared to be unpopular, which is never helpful in an election year, especially since it is by no means certain that he thinks he *is* unpopular. Prosperity has gone and won't come back just by wishing for it, and without prosperity to fall back on, the Republicans are in an almost hopeless position.

The only bond which remains to them is the bond of party. They have the morale which goes with continued power and responsibility. They have the habit of victory and it will take more than statistics and hot air to put them out of office. They have the habit of team play and the tradition of generations of patriotic Americans behind them. Win or lose, they can be counted on to fight it out to the finish and to profit by any mistake on the part of their opponents. Even if you don't like them, you've got to admire them for their skill in co-operation, by which they have repeatedly marshaled discordant forces to final victory, in the teeth of disaster.

In 1932, however, the breakdown in party spirit is so serious that it will require real political audacity to prevent a great defeat. When General Shafter's badly equipped little army lay before Santiago, its situation was so desperate that only a precipitate retreat could avert disaster. By a happy inspiration, the Americans demanded the surrender of the Spanish Army, and got it. Only strategic insanity of this order can prevent a nation-wide desertion of angry voters to the Democratic side. Can Hoover's 21,000,000 votes be kept in line? Can the bankrupt and desperate farmers, who hold the balance of power between the parties, be kept from whoring after strange political gods? Can the raging thirst of the beer belt be slaked without giving mortal offense to self-righteous Kansas and holier-than-thou Idaho? Can the disconsolate resentment of the bread lines and the soup kitchens be averted from the Party of Prosperity and the steady drift towards socialism, both inside and outside of the party, be challenged without driving the liberals into the Democratic camp? Has the party organization the brains and the power to master a national crisis?

In this particular, the Republicans are better off than the Democrats, whose Presidential campaign is pretty much a one-man show. The Republican Party is bigger than its leaders and organized so as to give the President control of essentials; the steam-roller tactics of the conservatives, coupled with the black and tan delegates from the rotten Republican boroughs of the Solid South, suffice to hold the Republican Convention in line. Such tactics in 1912, however, split the party and the latter, like the elephant which is its symbol, is able to learn by experience. The question of who controls the party will be decided by the delegates themselves, without coercion, and the President will be content with the rôle of party leader rather than party dictator. Aside from the right to name the Chairman of the National Committee and the obligation of the National Committee to support him during the campaign, the President has no lasting power over that famous and hard-boiled organization. To be sure, he has his advisers—men like Ray Benjamin who tell him what he ought to do and men like Senator Fess and Secretary Wilbur who tell him what he wants to do—but in the main the Republican National Committee is the real power of the party and constitutes an experienced and continuing organization, which would survive Hoover's defeat and still live to fight another day. And behind all work a small group of practical politicians and business men who make and unmake Presidents, policies and destinies without caring a damn for the fine feelings of idealists or the personal fortunes of individual candidates. The whole is knit into a centralized and efficient organization of political power which gives substance to the proud Republican claim that they are "the only party fit to govern."

Their great weakness is that they have no new policy to fit to a changed world. They are the party of production in a world which is worried by the problem of consumption. They are the party of nationalism in a world which realizes the need for internationalism. They came into power as a radical party with a national program,

all of which has been in effect for years. For generations
the slave-holding Democrats of the South had refused
the public domain to the white farmers of the North
and had blocked all moves for a protective tariff. The
farmers and the manufacturers joined hands, formed a
party, won an election, gave the farmers their land and
the industries their tariff, and have held to that line ever
since. Just to make sure that the alliance would last, the
Democrats were fools enough to force a Civil War on
the nation, were beaten after four years of ruinous fighting, and left the Republicans with a semi-monopoly of
patriotism for thirty years.

Finally, after the World War, the Republicans added
one more element to their alliance—labor. They began
restricting immigration (machinery having taken the
place of cheap labor) and have now practically throttled
it, thereby protecting the third big element in national
production against foreign competition. But a policy
achieved soon loses its sex appeal. The ardor of the electorate soon cools when it is discovered that the Democrats are only too eager to fondle the farmer, that they
are not at all anxious to establish free trade, and that,
far from welcoming immigrants to America, they are
more anti-foreign in matters of race, color and religion
than are the Republicans. Apparently, popular inertia
alone has prevented the Republican rank and file from
flirting with the Democratic machine. Yet the morale
and prestige of a great national party is not easily de-

stroyed, even by national adversity; those who reckon that the voter is swayed only by monetary considerations may be surprised by the political behavior of the Americans in a crisis; and, despite all auguries and logic, the Republicans may triumph overwhelmingly on the issue of swapping horses when crossing a stream.

For the Republicans can offer one priceless asset to a troubled nation: the party is bigger than its candidates. The Republicans have nominated and elected some of the least magnetic and brilliant of Presidents—men like Hayes and Harrison—and have still managed to give the country a pretty good administration. The party has survived the frauds and scandals of the Grant and Harding administrations, has survived three panics before this one, and has always come up smiling. In the process, the party managers have become our most skillful politicians, when operating on a national scale. Tammany can give them odds in a municipal election, plenty of Democratic state machines can run circles around them in an off year; but in a national election, the Republicans are in their element.

They are masters of electioneering and know to a nicety which prejudice will arouse the public at any given time. For a generation after the Civil War, they waved the "Bloody Shirt" in all elections, with the statement (which happened to be largely true) that "while not every Democrat was a Rebel, every Rebel was a Democrat." In the 'Nineties they seized on the national dread of anarchists and bombs to destroy Bryan's bold marriage of the Populists and the Democrats, and represented the Democratic campaign for free silver as "a campaign against the Ten Commandments." In the election of 1920, they appealed to every nationalistic prejudice which had been alarmed by Wilson's internationalism, and won the greatest popular majority in our history. In 1924, the Progressive movement under La Follette enabled them to appeal to the fear of political radicalism and the distrust of complicated politics which is the most notable feature of our post-war mood. In 1928, they did not hesitate to capitalize the religious and racial prejudices of the native Americans against the Catholic candidate from our immigrant Irish stock.

What prejudice can they successfully invoke in 1932? The Democrats are too wary to be caught again on the religious issue. There will be no Progressive Republican Party as in 1924. The anti-European appeal of 1920 won't wash when the Republicans are being forced to pursue an international policy on war debts and to cooperate with the League of Nations in the Far East. Under the circumstances, the Republicans may well be tempted to turn back in their memory book to the anti-Bryan campaign and to base their attack on the subversive social unrest which is the product of depression and of Soviet Russia. Fear of Bolshevism, hatred of communism, our traditional racial distrust of Russia would appear to offer the party demagogues their best chance of victory, short of involving the country in a foreign war.

With the South regarding membership in a labor union as an all but capital offense; with the union leaders themselves dreading the capture of the labor movement by the radicals; with our farmers irritated by Russian grain exports and our industrialists worried by the specter of a Planned Economy on the model of the Soviet Five-Year Plan; with the Catholic hierarchy committed to the overthrow of Marxian materialism; with a winter of ghastly unemployment, distress and radical proposals fresh in public memory, the Republicans may snuff up the East Wind which blows from Moscow and stake the success of their campaign on a titanic struggle to prevent the Bolshevization of America. The British Conservative Party has set the example; the world is swinging rapidly towards reactionary nationalism; and if the Democrats nominate a liberal or toy with proposals for the dole or for an American Five-Year Plan, the Republican Party managers may crash through with another staggering majority.

If re-elected, the party will commit the country to a new lease of nationalism. Our timid gestures towards international co-operation and disarmament will be discreetly laid aside. Our navy will be strengthened and the tariff maintained at a high level, while the United States reverts to its traditional policy of isolation, cutting its losses in Europe and blaming the foreigner very loudly and sincerely for everything that goes wrong. The party itself will continue to maintain its morale, train its leaders, administer the country, hold the offices, get the contracts and disburse the national payroll.

And all the time it will drift closer and closer to the split between the East and the West which is the next development in the course of political education. For the alliance between the farmer, the manufacturer and the laborer is too artificial to last. As the South becomes industrialized and as the westerners forget that they once regarded a farm as a desirable possession and not as an excuse for demanding more and more of the East's money, the party ties will snap. The protest votes will mount higher and higher in each election and the Republicans of the East and West, as well as the Democrats, will be unable indefinitely to use national or racial prejudices to prevent men from voting in accordance with their interests and ideas.

For a political revolution is taking place. Since the beginning of the century, the independent vote, which was ridiculous and contemptible in the pre-McKinley era, has become more than respectable. It is becoming decisive. It is now the vote which wins elections and changes administrations. This vote will decide the fate of both parties in 1932 and will determine whether the Republicans still have the brains and the skill to govern the country which they have dominated ever since the Democrats fired on the American flag at Fort Sumter.

VIII

The Protest Vote

I F FRANKLIN ROOSEVELT, Colonel House, or Mr. John
J. Raskob are gambling on getting the independent
vote of protest against hard luck and hard times, in order
to win the election, they are playing with the most dangerous sort of political dynamite. The independent vote
may decide elections, but it does not always decide them
the way it wants. A protest vote has a way of calling out
an answering vote of panic from the large unexplored
regions of the electorate that do not bother to cast a
ballot more than once in a lifetime. In the wild election of 1928, more than thirty-six million votes were
cast—a record; yet this was only a little more than half
of the qualified electors in the United States. If you sub-
tract the black men who aren't allowed to vote, the aliens
who can't vote, and the people who don't bother to vote
because they live in a "sure" state, you still have a margin
of at least twenty million votes which will never be cast
unless they are badly frightened.

That is what makes politicians as timid and secretive as
an old maid undressing in a strange bedroom. They adjust their policies to the well-established conventional

party lines and play safe within the limits of the machine. They would be as embarrassed if everyone voted as the Vatican would be if all the Protestants clamored to be taken into the Catholic Church or as Congress would be if Canada demanded to be annexed to the United States.

Now the pure party vote is strictly limited. It runs to about 17,000,000 for the Republicans and not more than 12,000,000 for the Democrats. With this set-up, the normal independent vote of about 5,000,000 is powerless to work much damage. These five millions lack a leader and lack an organization. In 1932 they will be looking for leadership and will grab the first man who looks as though he knows where he is going. Only twice in a generation have they found a man who really appealed to them: Roosevelt in 1912 and La Follette in 1924. Each time they cast their millions into the ballot box and each time they won the election—for somebody else.

For the protest vote is calculated to frighten the average American into fits. When faced with a radical movement his instinct is to go back and touch first base. The soreheads, the lunatic fringe, the Single Taxers, the parlor pinks, the mugwumps, liberals, radicals, the broke and the hungry are not the stuff of which a successful party is constructed. All they can do is to play merry hell with the regular parties. They may do so in 1932.

The independent voters find the country in a thoroughly angry mood. They realize that the government

guessed wrong about Russia, bet wrong on the stock
market, bet wrong on the tariff and prosperity, and
probably bet wrong on the World War. Certainly, if
Wilson had remained too proud to fight in 1917, the war
would have been over much sooner, fewer people would
have been killed, there would have been fewer debts to
pay, and lower taxes to pay them with. The thirty-seven
billions we spent on the Great Crusade could have been
saved and we would have been spared all this business
about war debts and reparations and who won the war
and why. As it is, the farmers have gone broke and our
industries have turned loose seven million wage-earners
to walk the streets and sample the spiritual values of
rugged individualism. Socialism is becoming respectable
and every established party faces revolt. This year the
protest vote may run as high as ten million irritated men
and women. At least that many will go to the ballot box
determined to register their disgust with things as they
are; their great difficulty will be to make their votes
count for things as they should be.

In other words, for whom can a protest-voter vote?
Not for Herbert Hoover, for he is the symbol of what
is wrong with the country. There remain only the Socialist and Democratic Parties; each offers a chance to
register thumbs-down on the Republican Administration. Either or both may offer a short-cut to the millen-
nium or a panacea for political gastritis, economic
chilblains and financial anemia.

Socialism is becoming dangerously respectable. Hitherto the Socialist vote has never passed the million mark. Of course, some of that is due to the old Tammany proverb: "I care not who may cast my country's votes, so long as I may count them." Even so, Socialism never appealed to Americans in the past. There were too many foreigners and Jews mixed up in it. Gentle Eugene Debs, the perennial Socialist candidate for President, went the rounds every four years and burbled about roses, but behind him were masses of hooked noses, curly hair and names ending in "baum," "stein," "sky," and "ovitch." It never stood a chance outside of a few places like Milwaukee and certain districts in New York City, where Morris Hillquit's brilliant but futile campaigns simply emphasized the fact that so long as Tammany counted the votes there wasn't much use in voting the radical ticket.

All that has changed. The party is becoming Americanized. With unusual sagacity, it has put at its head a Protestant clergyman—the Rev. Dr. Norman Thomas, a handsome, earnest, and highly respectable figure. The party attracted the interest of the intelligentsia when Heywood Broun, the inexhaustible columnist, ran for Congress on the Socialist ticket in 1930. In 1931, the party had gone so far that in the local New York elections some disgusted Republican leaders urged their followers to vote for the Socialist candidate instead of the regular Republican. This is a far cry from the day when the Republicans and Democrats joined forces to keep Henry George, the Single-Taxer, from becoming Mayor of New York. As both of the major parties drift around in the vicious circle of political paralysis, young professional men are being attracted into the Socialist camp. Dr. Thomas goes solemnly about the country, lecturing, exhorting, debating the merits of capitalism with a reactionary like Hamilton Fish, and the Socialist Party, purified, naturalized and disinfected of its alien taint, can depend on two or three million votes (when, as, and if counted) in the next election.

Those who want to take a crack at Hoover and who don't want to vote Socialist, must vote Democratic and will do so, if the Democrats give them half a chance. This means that, to the normal 12,000,000 Democratic votes may be added 7,000,000 independent votes, while at least 3,000,000 of Hoover's phenomenal 21,000,000 may switch to the Democratic candidate. This little sum in political arithmetic, therefore, works out—and this is what Colonel House expects—as follows: Democrats —22,000,000; Republicans—18,000,000, which would be very nice for the Democrats.

It would not be so pleasant for Mr. Hoover and his Republican supporters. If Hoover is beaten in 1932 he is through; the Republicans waste neither time nor sympathy over unsuccessful candidates. If he wants to avoid going into the school-books as a Presidential panic, he has got to win here and now. If he plays his cards well, he can use the protest vote to ruin his Democratic opponent. The formula is simple. The Democrats must nominate either a liberal or a conservative, a Roosevelt or a Ritchie. Suppose they decide to gamble on picking up the support of the sore-heads. They then choose Roosevelt and hang out the latch-string to the radicals. Thereupon, the Republicans, as in 1896, discover that not the Party but the Nation is in danger. They accuse the Democrats of having sold out to anarchy; they call Roosevelt a communist and his platform rankest Bolshevism. They frighten every farmer, worker and manufacturer out of his wits, strike up the "Star-Spangled Banner," and turn out a panic vote which runs the Republican score up to 28,000,000 and leaves the Democrats, with all their gains, still trailing by five or six million beans. Which would be very sad for Colonel House, the Roosevelt rooters, and the Democratic party.

"Aha!" says Mr. Raskob. "We aren't such fools as to fall into *that* trap." So he calls the wiser heads of the party together, points out the peril, tells them to stick to some safe-and-sane gentleman like Ritchie, or Owen Young, or Melvin Traylor, the Texas-Chicago banker who represents Mr. Morgan on the World Bank at Basle, and who can be trusted not to attract the liberals. Mr. Raskob figures that in this way, Mr. Hoover will lose three million disgusted followers, that about half of the bellyachers will go Democratic, and that the Socialists must be let severely alone. That works out as a neat little Democratic total of 20,000,000 to a depressing Republican 18,000,000—a result extremely pleasing to Mr. Raskob and most depressing to the earnest Mr. Hoover.

This time, however, the protest vote, annoyed at being expected to choose between an Owen Young and a Herbert Hoover, starts furiously in the direction of Norman Thomas, uttering loud cries of rage. Bruce Bliven of *The New Republic,* Oswald Garrison Villard of *The Nation,* solemnly urge their readers to vote Socialist as a way of registering their contempt for both candidates. Prominent young gentlemen like Hamilton Hadley, the sons of respectable Republican parents, suddenly come out for Socialism and graciously consent to run for Congress in some hopeless district. Then the Republicans profess great alarm. They say that they regard Dr. Norman Thomas as their real adversary and they proceed to ignore entirely the eloquent and learned speeches of Mr. Young or Governor Ritchie. As in 1924, they suggest that the election may be thrown into Congress and profess fear of the terrible uncertainty for business which would result from this feature of our Constitution, which is otherwise so admirable. They inform the country that the real menace is the Socialist Party, that behind Socialism is Bolshevism, and that Stalin is back of Dr. Thomas, just as the Pope was back of Al Smith. They frighten everybody, including some of the Democrats, so thoroughly that when all the figures are in it is discovered that 3,000,000 radicals voted for Norman Thomas, that 16,000,000 marked the Democratic ticket, and that 23,000,000 suckers decided to answer the margin call on Herbert Hoover. It would all be very patriotic.

Properly handled, the 1932 election is a sure thing for the Republicans. All the Democratic calculations are based on what happened in the last election and what can be done with the last Presidential vote of thirty-six millions. The Republicans have it in their power to bring out a panic vote of over forty millions, and to turn the protest vote against the Democrats, if they are willing to let a few hard-boiled old pirates like Senator Moses of New Hampshire and Ray Benjamin of California run the show. The only trouble with such demagoguery is that it does not remove the cause of the protest vote and therefore cannot be used twice in the same depression.

For all of the protest vote is not based on sheer wrong-headedness. It is the product of damnably stupid business and political methods. The old statement about millions starving in the midst of plenty has been worked to death, but it is still true and the moral problem of our civilization remains unanswered. It is scandalous that the wealthiest country in the world should be unable to secure the necessities of life for all its people, that only a tenth of our population can obtain modest comfort; and it is sheer insanity that such a country should be unable to provide for the fifth of its population which is hit by unemployment except by passing the hat around, while the business system which produced the mess refuses to submit to any form of effective control. If it is true, as Chairman Stone of the Farm Board said, that a further drop of two cents in the price of wheat in November, 1930, would have destroyed the financial structure of the country, then there is something radically wrong with our entire system. When, after more than two years of panic and depression, the voters see that the high-pressure boys of the big business world—men like Silas Strawn of Chicago, Thomas Lamont of Morgan's, and Henry Ford—have absolutely nothing to offer in the way of a practical remedy for this condition (except home-gardening), are we to be blamed for thinking that direct, radical political action offers about the only hope of improvement?

The protest vote is really the first installment of the future. We know that it will do no good in 1932, will elect no significant candidates, change nothing at the time when change is needed. But it will give the major parties their ideas for the future. Once an idea wins popular support, it is quickly adopted by politicians who are hunting votes. For a politician to believe that an idea has popular support, he must see people vote for it. Otherwise it is just talk, and talk is cheap. The Populists in the '90's and the Progressives in 1912 had policies, radical, "impractical" and dangerous policies, and they voted for them. Now, if you look at our statute books you will find that practically everything they demanded —the income tax, direct primaries, popular election of senators, woman suffrage, postal savings and such—has become the law of the land.

For this reason, the historian of the future and the editor of the present—even the venerable Mr. Rollo Ogden of *The New York Times* and the pugnacious and omniscient Mr. Arthur Brisbane of the Hearst press —are invited to consider carefully the platform of the Socialist Party in 1932. Its candidates will not be elected. Its votes may not even be counted, and if they are, will only confuse and distort the issue to the advantage of the Republicans. But what it recommends in 1932 will probably be the law of the land in another twenty years.

IX

This Damned Depression

HARD times is the only issue in which the American people are interested in 1932. "Interested" is scarcely the word, for they are fighting-mad and already the more diseased minds of our vindictively radical sociologists are threatening all those who differ with them on any minute point in the solution of the challenge of over-production and unemployment, with excommunication by the Soviet and with physical extinction.

The four horsemen of the Red Revolution are riding and the beat of the pale hooves echoes like thunder in the bankers' vaults, while the wind of their passing scatters our prettily colored paper securities like autumn leaves before a gale. Whether the wild riders of hunger and debt, unemployment and despair, pass us by this time or harrow this land for the greater glory of Marx, is another matter. Terrible thoughts are in the air and as evictions tumble hopeless families into the streets, as children shiver and men mutter at the street corners, the undertow of revolution palsies the strongest swimmer in our economic tides and swamps statesmanship in the waves of panic and panacea. Private charity falters, government faces deficit, debt, and taxes, and with material wealth in abundance our society lacks the will or the brains to prevent hardship and to preserve hope against the future. Millions of Americans, employed and unemployed, are stirring from their civic trance and, despite all the thimblerigging of politicians, are preparing to resort to the ballot, for change or for revenge.

Whatever hard times may mean to the nation or the individual, to the politician they spell opportunity. Never a President or a party in the last century has survived a panic. Hard times in 1920 toppled the Democrats from office so brutally that it took them eight years to realize what had happened. Now both Republican and Democratic politicians are wondering whether the situation has become so desperate that the election of a Democratic President is warranted. If things start to mend, the Republicans may come back. If they continue as at present, the Democrats will win. If they are so bad that there is no hope of recovery for several years, the Republicans would prefer to let the Democrats take the blame and the terrible responsibilities of office during the remaining years of the depression.

There is no blinking the fact that our political and economic leadership has broken down. Where are the supermen of yesteryear? Gone, all are gone, with the price of common stocks and the theory of high wages. Not one of our "great" bankers, "great" industrialists, "great" economists or financial "experts" has survived the bull-market. Neither Morgan nor Ford nor Otto Kahn nor Professor Kemmerer nor Irving Fisher is selling at the old high. We have serious unemployment—the worst in our history—seven million men out of work at present, and, apart from charity, we have no national means of keeping them alive, clothed, warmed and fed. Wage cut after wage cut has destroyed the purchasing power of the masses. Foreign markets—that old refuge of the depressed industrialist—are closing like clams, as every nation puts itself in a state of economic siege and endeavors to sell more than it buys. Bread lines and soup kitchens are not a perfect solution of the worst problem of the twentieth century. The dehumanization of energy, the shift from coal to oil and from oil to electricity, the perfection of automatic machinery and the substitution of chemistry for natural produce, has robbed the race of the ownership of its tools, while the multiplication of corporations and the inflation of prices and of capital have robbed the rich of the rewards of wealth. We have created a machine which does not consume capital or labor in proportion to its ability to create wealth. For a time, with high wages, installment selling, and forced-draft stock-market speculation, we hid our faces in the sand. Now they are being ground in the dirt, as we discover that we have neglected to enable the people to acquire the wealth created by our own machinery. It is a bitter situation. If only we could see to it that everybody had a regular supply of little slips of colored paper to exchange for what he needs, we think that all would be well. In the meantime, nine-tenths of our people are in poverty and men drop dead of starvation —although "malnutrition" looks prettier in the medical reports—every day in our bread lines. No wonder that the man who is out of work today, he who may be out of work tomorrow, as well as the one whose pay has been cut by edict from on high, feels angry.

Angry, too, are the farmers, who are suffering because they have produced too much. They shiver because they have raised too much food and burn their corn for fuel, while miners starve in the eastern coal fields because nobody can buy their coal. Too much wheat, too much cotton, the lowest prices in our history, foreclosure of mortgages, added to the perils of flood, drought, boll-weevil, corn-borer and locust, have enraged the inhabitants of the Mississippi Basin to a degree in which they are capable of anything.

New competition from Russia, from the Argentine, from Canada, Australia, Africa; new machinery, new processes in textiles, rayon, cotton-fields in India, Nigeria and the Sudan: all have conspired to rob the American farmer of his foreign markets. China in chaos, Russia under the Soviets, India seething with sedition, half the human race in a state of political and economic disorganization; Europe so threatened with war or revolution that every nation makes shift to grow its own food against an emergency: the risks of American farming have expanded to include the risks of world politics in an era when world affairs are threatened with complete demoralization. New modes of agricultural production: the industrial farm of the prairies, the Russian collective farm, the peonage of the South, the croppers, all are combining to drive the small farmer off the soil just at the time when the industrial hangover is driving the workless out of the cities. On the one hand, fear of communism fostered by the city unemployed; on the other, fear of dispossession fostered by debt—the farmer is desperate and weighs the future with the suspicious hatred characteristic of the rural mind whenever confronted with the new and strange.

Third and most absurd member in our trinity of economic despair are the bankers. Pity the poor bankers. For a generation, they have pretended to a holier-than-thou prominence in business matters. For them the headlines have hushed, steam yachts and Follies girls have been launched, Florida palaces and royal suites have been reserved. Now they are exposed as boobs on an all but cosmic scale, when an Owen Young "settles" the reparations question for all time on the eve of the world's greatest panic, when a Charley Mitchell loads the National City up on South American bonds and a Wiggin pours the cash of the Chase National into Germany just in time to get caught by the swinging doors. Banks are failing, profits are dwindling, life insurance companies and savings banks are demanding artificial breathing and injections of credit in order to prevent "gilt-edged" bonds from expiring on their hands. International capitalism has made a ghastly mess of its opportunities.

The world's credit structure has been caught by the house detectives emerging from the wrong room at the wrong hour. Billions of American dollars have been sent overseas and drained away into sterile political and commercial loans. Money has been loaned to enable governments to balance budgets, pay debts, cities to build stadia and model dwellings, foreign industries to duplicate factories already existing in the United States. Money has been loaned to enable foreigners to buy American goods without the necessity of selling anything in return. Billions have been siphoned into Germany in order to finance the payment of reparations imposed by force and war debts repudiated in spirit, without even making sure that, in a show-down, these loans would not be tangled in the fly paper of Europe's political financial arrangements. Millions have been loaned to insecure dictators and anti-democratic governments in Europe and South America. With the British Empire, Africa, Asia and Russia clamoring for capital with which to develop their natural resources, our "big" bankers have risked the savings of a generation on the lousiest set of political loans ever floated since the Fuggers attempted to finance the death-throes of the Holy Roman Empire.

England has gone off the gold standard and the major part of world trade is crippled by the risks of depreciating currency. France hurls her lance of gold against the enemies of the Treaty of Versailles, and in the United States, with the greatest gold supply in human history, our entire credit structure has been sapped by unwise loans to insolvent foreigners and by the impossibility of balancing a huge pyramid of debt on a shifting heap of gold. The bankers are in a desperate position. Men have dangled from lamp-posts or have faced firing-squads for lesser follies and imprudences with the welfare of other people. Some bankers run away. Some go to prison. Some jump out of lofty buildings. Some simply watch the ticker and wish that the earth would open up and swallow them. A few—a very few—have the nerve, the brains, or the stubbornness to see the thing through. The rest are pitiable fools who didn't know it was loaded, any more than did the veriest sucker to whom they sold worthless stock at a high price in 1929.

Of course, this is only a partial picture of affairs. The times are not so hard as they seem: they couldn't be. The visible economic machinery of mankind has broken down but that doesn't mean that economic life has stopped. The great mass of our people eat, sleep, marry, beget children, produce, buy and sell, and life goes on and on and on. It always has and always will, so long as the planet is reasonably habitable and as long as courage and hope are bred into the average human being. Nevertheless, we don't and can't see that side of the picture; what we don't know can't help us; and what we do know and see and hear is that we are having hard times. The result is that the election has become a race between prosperity and the ballot box, with all the odds on the ballot box.

Hence, depression is the unescapable issue in the 1932 campaign. It doesn't matter whether the rival parties talk about the Einstein theory or the Eighteenth Amendment, birth control or the parking problem; the issue will be the depression. As a matter of fact, it will be discussed, if not by the major parties, at least by the Socialists and the Communists. America owes the Communists one great debt on that score: until the workless demonstrations of March, 1930, our politicians refused to admit that there was such a thing as serious unemployment in this country. It is painful to consider what might have happened if that Pollyanna mood had lasted for another six months; it's quite bad enough as it is.

Of course, both parties will have to mention the depression. Neither will be overanxious to do so. The Democrats will say that the election of their candidate will bring back prosperity. The Republicans will say that it would retard the return of prosperity to change horses while crossing the stream. Neither side will be very specific about how to get prosperity. They will gamble on its coming back through natural causes, knowing perfectly well that neither can do anything about it. Hence the Socialists and Communists will be the political heirs of the epidemic of Plans which has swept the country since the time when Russia's inconvenient exports made us conscious of the Five-Year Plan. Neither big party is yet ready to accept the shocking idea that it might be a good scheme to know exactly what you are trying to do with your business system if you really wish to avoid overproduction and unemployment. Accordingly, the big parties will pass by on the other side when they come to Economic Planning and will accept the more congenial job of acting as traffic cops in the rush for the Treasury.

For if one idea has registered a bull's-eye with our politically organized classes it is that the government should pay all the bills which our reckless business system ran up during its last debauch. He who challenges the dogma that the taxpayer shall be made to pay for the blunders of our hit-and-run business system will be regarded as a traitor to the people, and he who sees that the idea of making the dinosaurs of the income tax pay it all is merely a revival of the vicious old Roman system of tax-farming will be denounced as a black reactionary.

The drive for Federal Unemployment Relief will be all but irresistible. The farmers, led by Senator Brookhart, are already demanding a billion dollars more from the Treasury in order to raise prices to the consumer at the consumer's expense. The veterans are ganging up for another bonus raid, this time for a couple of billions, on Ogden Mills's cash-register. And the government faces a two-billion-dollar deficit at the end of the fiscal year. Hearst wants a five-billion-dollar "Prosperity Loan" at a time when the government had hard sledding in floating its last issue. The railroads are demanding higher rates and lower wages; the banks are demanding a ten-billion-dollar bonus in the shape of cancellation of war debts at the expense of the tax-payer; the industries are demanding help in the form of emancipation from the anti-trust laws—and it is highly amusing to note that the "conservative" institutions of this country are just as eager for the "dole"—whether it be called a tariff, a subsidy, a loan, freedom from law or taxes—as are the unworthy and impractical "radicals" who simply want cash for the individual. To offset and meet this demand, there will be an all but resistless demand for inflation: for free silver, for currency bonds, for printing-press money, and only a half-dozen unpopular vetoes by poor President Hoover will stand between the deflated consumer and high taxes and cheap money, between the United States and fiscal anarchy.

So you can't keep hard times out of the election. They are here and even if the Republicans pull a vest-pocket boom or an economic miracle before election day, the memory of hard times will still be with the voter. It will give the political patience and the economic common-sense of our people the most searching test they have had in forty years. We shall have to decide whether the election of 1932 is to be the first step towards socialism—no matter how it is labeled—or a curtain raiser for an

American revolution such as that which Andrew Jackson headed a century ago. The decision will be the more momentous because, no matter whether a Democrat, a Republican, or a Socialist enters the White House, hard times are not going to pass until we discover that the secret of prosperity is intelligence, co-operation and social purpose, rather than capitalistic greed, revolutionary emotion or cussed human prejudice. We don't even know the alphabet of the economic language of the future. On the day when America learns that what we sell impoverishes us while what we buy enriches us, we shall have commenced our A.B.C. If you think we have learned that lesson—look at our tariff. If, on the other hand, you think we are incapable of learning it, look at our triumphant organization of production. Any nation which has our capacity for producing will sooner or later learn how to consume. However, it will take more than the angry votes of unemployed or impoverished men to teach us the art of conquering hard times, which is simply the art of living.

X

Drink and the Devil

INASMUCH as horrified indignation at the sinfulness of someone else has always characterized the American people, those who hope to turn the election of 1932 into a free fight about the liquor question, with the Drys wailing about the evils of alcohol and the Wets deploring the rise of the beer-barons and the racketeers, have much in their favor. It would be quite typical of the utter abandon of American politics if an election which will affect our entire future mode of existence and which will lead to a new conception of the government's rôle in business, should be fought on the issue of the repeal of the Eighteenth Amendment. Hence, whatever the object of the battle for control at Washington, the battle-cry is apt to be intensely alcoholic.

Prohibition has about as much chance of being repealed as a result of this Presidential election as the average American has of becoming President. As one of the Wickersham Commission was heard to remark, "The damn thing is in the Constitution!" A new President can't repeal it, Congress can't repeal it, a majority of the people can't repeal it. Thirteen states in the sheep-tick and boll-weevil regions, with a population equal to a single Eastern state, have the Constitutional power to prevent repeal. The Drys worked for twenty years to put it over and they were helped by a World War; the Wets will have to work hard and long to pull the Methodist Amendment out of the Constitution. Hence Prohibition as a practical political issue is utterly irrelevant to the decision of who will be who at Washington.

As a battle cry, however, the subject is hard to beat. Everybody feels strongly about it; everybody that wants to drink has a little trouble in buying or brewing it; the damn law has never worked and obviously never will; the whole idea of controlling the commercialized traffic in alcoholic beverages has been lost in the shuffling of religious and sectional manias. The subject has all the makings of a first-class controversy and in 1932 it will afford politicians excellent excuse for side-stepping the real question of the day—hunger rather than thirst.

The case for Prohibition is very simple. Alcohol is a dangerous and habit-forming drug. So long as the brewers and distillers had a selfish interest in expanding their sales, all attempts to control the retail traffic of the saloon, by taxes, by licenses, by local option and by special legislation, broke down. Poverty, disease, prostitution and unrest were by-products of the legalization of alcoholism. To attempt to destroy the profit element in the liquor traffic by outlawing the traffic itself was "a great social and economic experiment, noble in motive."

DRINK AND THE DEVIL

The mass of the people are better off without it; Prohibition has given us prosperity; labor saves its wages (when it gets any) to buy food and furniture, radios and automobiles; wives and children get clothed and fed more regularly if men can't blow their week's wages at the corner saloon; real estate values rise and a dangerous focus where ignorant men can exchange their immature political ideas and thus combine against their employers and against "the decent element" has been done away with.

The case against Prohibition is just as simple. The mass of our people did not and do not drink to excess and to forbid them to drink in moderation is an act of tyranny. Our race has been drinking alcohol since the dawn of history; no teetotal civilization has ever amounted to anything; we don't know what dangerous forces we may release when we cease exposing human tissues to the toughening and selective action of a racial poison. If we wished to strike at the commercialized traffic in alcohol, to destroy the sales urge to make drunkards of us all, there are other and better ways of doing it. We cannot regulate or control a traffic which has no legal existence. Usually men are not poor because they drink, more often they drink because they are poor and because drink is the poor man's short cut to happiness. The relationship between alcohol and disease is not proven, especially since the world's most vital and tenacious races are without exception alcoholic. Prostitution is the by-product of the money basis of society rather than of the saloon. Quite as many girls take the easiest way in the back seats of parked automobiles as ever went the way of all flesh in the back-rooms of corner-saloons. To attempt to proscribe human appetite is a stupid trifling with human nature, which positively challenges violation of the law. To attempt to induce prosperity by outlawing drink is to adopt a childish view of economics, to regard money rather than goods as the basis of wealth, and hence is an absurdity, as though we could add to our wealth by refusing to permit the production of wealth, i.e. of goods for which there is a demand. On the same argument, we would be tremendously enriched if we outlawed the automobile—with its annual casualties, its waste of our natural resources and its disrupting influence upon home life and church attendance.

Fear of the saloon is simply fear of democracy, distrust of drink is simply distrust of the average American citizen. We are not children who must be forbidden to put certain liquids into our mouths or certain ideas into our heads. Self-government has broken down when the political organization of our country is such that a small minority can forbid the majority of our citizens to meet, drink and talk under the stimulus of a convenient drug which overcomes shyness and promotes expansive and generous ideas. For our political health and our individual self-respect we must get rid of the prohibitory system which has fostered hypocrisy, crime and disrespect for

law, and which has financed the criminal classes by di-
verting to them the profits of a traffic which is rooted in
human nature and racial habit.

In theory, the two view-points on Prohibition are
fairly balanced; in practice, after twelve years of Messrs.
Capone and the lawless thugs and grafters of the Prohibition Unit, the case against Prohibition is pretty well
proved. The law does not work in America and it's time
to change it. The politicians, however, do not dare do
anything real about it. The issue is too good a boob-
tickler to be thrown away. Also the forces of the Drys
and Wets, if openly opposed, would punish any politician who met the issue honestly. A comparative handful
of votes may hold the balance between victory and defeat in any congressional district and a Congressman's
first duty is to get himself elected. If he doesn't do that,
he isn't a Congressman.

The practical solution is, accordingly, simple nullification. Don't offend the Drys by trying to change the law.
Don't offend the Wets by trying to enforce it. The bootleggers have arrived and have the situation well in hand.
No man with the price need go thirsty long in this moral
country. It is easy to brew beer in your own home; there
is a flourishing and rather legal business in selling innocent grape-juice which, when properly "serviced," becomes high-test wine. This product, under the name of
Vine-Glo, or other Volsteadian trade-marks, is vouched
for by none other than Mrs. Mabel Walker Willebrandt,

once the Joan of Arc of Prohibition enforcement, and is financed by the funds of the Federal Farm Board. All the shouting for 2.75 or 4% beer is the bunk. Who would drink such hogwash anyhow? Beer should contain at least 8% and wine 12% of alcohol. The really popular quick drinks—cocktails and highballs—are based on gin, rum and whisky of at least 40% alcoholic content. Congress could not modify the Volstead Act so as to permit a really intoxicating beverage without running into the Supreme Court and having the new law declared unconstitutional. If the President refuses to enforce the law he renders himself liable to impeachment. Under such circumstances, don't expect heroic behavior from Congressmen. If left to themselves, all they need do about the law is to refuse, in the name of economy, to appropriate money specially for its enforcement, just as Congress once refused to appropriate money for the enforcement of the Thirteenth, Fourteenth and Fifteenth Amendments—which attempted to free and enfranchise the Southern Negroes—after a prolonged and loudly moral attempt to work out the noble experiment of putting the black man in the saddle. The South did not object to that particular type of nullification; if the South objects to nullification of the Eighteenth Amendment, it will be just too bad. So the solution of Prohibition lies much nearer at hand than is generally assumed: within four years at the most.

This solution—nullification by non-appropriation—

will be necessary because Prohibition has twisted itself around the most robust passions of our political life. The Native Americans against the wine-bibbing Aliens; the pure Country against the sodden City; the manly West against the effeminate East; the pious South against the godless North; the wise employers against the improvident workers; the abstemious Protestants against the alcoholic Catholics; autocracy against democracy; the rich against the poor; the women against the men; these are the passions which you touch when you touch the liquor question. It is dynamite for a politician to touch one of these—to touch them all at once is like a Chinese New Year's celebration. In local elections, where the will of the community is clearly known in advance, the subject may be safe; in national elections it is taboo. Hence the recent enthusiasm for a referendum on the subject. That would change nothing, simply reveal how people felt without endangering a single candidate for public office. After the votes were counted, you would find the politicians discovering their own convictions.

If such a referendum had been held ten years ago, the country would have voted dry. Today, the chances are that the country would show itself overwhelmingly wet and for that reason the Drys have no enthusiasm for such a cheap way of informing a Congressman that it is safe to knife the Volstead Act. The straws which show the public feeling have all been wet. No longer are the Wets the representatives of breweries and distilleries, of saloon keepers and the underworld. No longer are the Drys the earnest Christian people, the women and the preachers, of America. The Wets of 1932 include the Federation of Labor, the Bar Association, the Medical Association, the American Legion, the Junior League, the Social Register, many of the clergy, the gentlewomen of America organized by Mrs. Sabin into the Repealist groups with nearly 500,000 members, the young gentlemen of America grouped in the Crusaders, and just about nine-tenths of all the young men and women who have come of age since the War.

The great support of Prohibition and some of the dry money undoubtedly comes from the bootleggers who are the beneficiaries of the present arrangement. The industrialists who believed that Prohibition was the Secret of Our Prosperity are now in the "Oh Yeah?" class. Only Henry Ford holds firm to the belief that it is better for a man to lose his whole soul if he saves enough to buy a Tudor sedan. Old men who got their ideas thirty, forty and fifty years ago; old women whose beauty is of the same vintage; political parsons like Bishop Cannon; southerners who want to keep the niggers from buying gin; super-efficiency employers who believe that if they hire a man's working hours they have bought his whole life; and the dwindling mass of self-righteous boobs who are too stubborn to admit that America could possibly make a major political blunder, are still on the side of the Amendment.

Most of our complacency has been shaken by the collapse of the prosperity which Prohibition was supposed to have created and by the explosion of scandals in practically every major city, by the baby-killing in New York, by Chicago, by the discovery that the principal effect of Prohibition has been to endow organized crime with the revenues of a government, to enable criminals to maintain private armies, to collect taxes from frightened shopkeepers, to convict and punish their enemies, and to negotiate political and business agreements throughout the country. The effrontery of Al Capone, who proposed a reasonable treaty with the Washington Government by which he should pay the Treasury for the national beer concession, coupled with the shabby subterfuge of prosecuting him for tax evasion, has shaken public confidence in the idea that nothing is too big for America to handle. Chicago has been hastily deodorized and New York's crime has been advertised by Mr. Seabury for the benefit of the Republican Party, but the bootleggers' trucks thunder over our highways, the rum fleets lie off our coasts, the smoke of ten thousand stills reeks to the sky, bathtub gin flows freely, Maryland farms yield forty gallons to the acre, our cities are pockmarked with speakeasies, enforcement officers still murder citizens with impunity, and policemen get rich very quickly on very small salaries. Prohibition has lost us our control of the liquor traffic and now we are paying the price.

WHAT WE ARE ABOUT TO RECEIVE

The election of 1932 won't settle the liquor problem and won't pour oil on the crime wave. The basis of crime is property and the basis of liquor is thirst, and Prohibition combines the worst features of both. However, no matter how we vote, Congress is not going to outlaw property or abolish thirst. The utmost that the politicians can do is to keep us interested in the subject of unsanctified thirst so that we won't have the time or the desire to monkey with sanctified property rights. They will let us talk about Prohibition, play with it, wallow in it, but they won't let us settle it—not this year.

XI

Peace at a Price

THE oldest trick in politics is to prevent trouble at home by making trouble abroad. The old formula to avoid a revolution is to wage a foreign war. The new American scheme is to distract the voters' attention from depression at home by pursuing world peace in a violent and unequivocal manner. So it happens that world peace is going to be an issue in the 1932 election; not that we will do anything about it but that the American people feel convinced that they have a monopoly on good intentions and can, somehow or other, persuade the other nations to behave themselves in a thoroughly moral manner. Never in our history have we been willing to pay the price of organized world peace, which is responsibility and self-control. We will never consent at the request of other nations, to scrap one single American policy— tariff, immigration or Prohibition—which makes for international ill will, and we will not pledge our wealth and lives to maintain such peace as exists outside of our sacred borders. Aside from that, we are all for peace, disarmament and good will among men.

The thousands of nice, well-meaning people throughout the country who believe in peace have votes, and it is worth while to please them. The pacifist racket is thoroughly organized and is in tune with the churches. We are never at a loss for ideals so long as Dr. Nicholas Murray Butler, Raymond Leslie Buell and Jimmy Macdonald of the Foreign Policy Association, Professor Shotwell and the Carnegie Foundation, Barney Baruch and the Institute of Politics, Laura Puffer Morgan, Dorothy Detzer, the Bok Foundation, the World Peace Foundation, the League of Nations Non-Partisan Association and the Federation of Churches of Christ in America, Inc. are on the job. This is a pity, because while ideals are all right, professional idealism is dangerous. Under the moral impact of these worthy propagandists and institutions, a gratuitous idealism has been one of our most conspicuous exports to the rest of the world, ever since the world discovered that we had money to lend. It is also a pity, because professional idealism, when trained on the many deplorable conditions outside of our borders, distracts our attention from the need for reform at home. There are people who weep more for one Russian refugee than for ninety-nine starving American coal miners and who shed hotter tears for one massacred Armenian than for a hundred lynched American Negroes. There are people who worry more about the size of the French Army than about the number of American unemployed and who regard the solvency of the German Reichsbank as more important than the solvency of the United States Treasury. This is the practical effect of the organized peace-minded groups upon American affairs. In 1932 they are to have their innings.

Never was world peace threatened so opportunely as today. The Japanese are making themselves at home in the Far East; in Latin America one revolution succeeds another and one bond issue after another is defaulted; Eastern and Central Europe are in ferment; France, Great Britain, Germany and Italy are in the grip of nationalism; Soviet Russia looms like a thunderhead to the East and profits by the bickerings of the capitalistic world. We alone are pure; we alone are disinterested; we alone are peaceful and peace-loving—we think. And all the time, for all the yelps of the Navy League, our cruisers slip down the ways, our aircraft drone through the heavens, our chemical warfare service improves our gases and explosives, and our economic and financial grip on the destinies of mankind is tightened. So we press forward to a disarmament conference which pretends that you can remove the causes of war by attacking the means of warfare, and the cares of the world wrinkle the brows of the apple-cheeked boys in the State Department who have discovered that the road to diplomatic advancement in America lies through the hot and continuous pursuit of international disarmament.

How long has this been going on? Wilson began it with his war to end war and its logical result in a peace to end peace. Europe's outstanding and typical prob-

lem, the Polish Corridor, with its threat of war or revolution, is the direct result of Wilson's single-handed fight
to give Poland an outlet to the sea through German
territory. One is amazed at America's official indiffer-
ence to the solution of this and a dozen other bitter
European controversies in the making of which our
diplomacy played a very large part. Nevertheless, since
the Treaty of Versailles we have been the world's great
holier-than-thou. We held the Washington Naval Conference of 1921-22, the Geneva Naval Conference of
1927, the London Naval Conference of 1930. We promoted the "settlement" of German reparations by the
Dawes Plan in 1924, the Young Plan in 1929, and the
Basle Conference in 1931. Now we are preparing, with
great moral flag-flapping, to make the Kellogg Pact of
1928 and the Manchurian row of 1931, an issue in a
domestic American election, and to demand that Europe
proceed with a disarmament agreement which will res-
urrect every European quarrel of the last twenty years.

The joke of it is that, in the meantime, there has
been a political revolution in the United States. The
Republicans who were elected in 1920 on a nationalistic "America First!" platform are now in full cry
after international co-operation, while the Democrats,
who were for the League of Nations in 1920, are now
adopting nationalism as a party policy. As the mass of
our people are violent nationalists without knowing it,
the Republicans have got on the unpopular side of the

issue. The American people really do not care a damn
for Europe. They mistrust Japan—the Yellow Peril—
and they have been taught to suspect Soviet Russia—
the Red Menace—in the Far East, but they aren't prepared to bleed and die for peace in China or in Europe
and they bitterly resent the occasional necessity to bleed
and die for peace in Central America and the Caribbean. In a show-down, the Americans would vote for
isolation in preference to any kind of world peace that
demanded their active physical support, and, so long as
there is no law against giving advice to people who
don't want it, will confine their pacifism to self-righteous and impractical suggestions to nations less fortu-
nately located, geographically and morally, than ourselves.

Hence, when any practical test is made of any of
the Great Moral Urges which inspire our statesmen and
inflate our Foreign Policy Association, Congress gives
the show away. The World Court is out of practical
American politics. Our membership in the League of
Nations is still an utter impossibility. Disarmament conferences have succeeded only to the extent to which we
were prepared to limit our own means of defense—
no other great power has been significantly weakened
as a result of all our peace palaver. The war debts—
the only brutal means we had of enforcing our will on
our European rivals—have been frittered away in controversy and in diplomacy. The Hoover Moratorium

and the attempted financial rescue of Central Europe leave as their net result the spectacle of indignant American tax-payers called upon to assume the burden of Europe's ten-billion-dollar debt to our Treasury. The Republican administration stole the stale Democratic thunder and .ran away with the "international issue" in American politics; if they are not careful, they will still be running on election day, as the Democrats become hard-boiled and uncharitable about these great moral gestures for which we have to foot the bill.

It is a pity that both parties will play domestic politics with our foreign policy, for the course of American diplomacy—though unpopular at home and bewildering abroad—has been leading us straight to world power. In the name of the highest principles, uttering the most impeccable platitudes, refining our notions with a Pharisaical expertness, we have been walking delicately towards the greatest measure of real power ever enjoyed by a modern nation, very much as a cat approaches a canary.

We have been washing our hands of the Caribbean, withdrawing our marines from Haiti and Nicaragua, explaining away the Monroe Doctrine, and establishing decent and tolerant relations with Mexico. In Manchuria, we have dimly sensed the possibility of calling the Red World into existence to redress the balance of the Yellow. We made a friendly gesture towards Russia in 1930, and in 1931 we tried to keep the peace between

Japan and China. If the Communists were not such damn fools and we were not so set in our opinions, we could have restored friendly relations with the Russian Government at any time in the last three years. But with Russia reading a war plot into the wheat purchases of the Federal Farm Board and with our armchair conservatives reading a revolutionary plot into Russian exports of grain and timber, there has been no chance of sane co-operation between the world's two great federal republics. Until there is such co-operation, world peace does not stand a chance; even without it, American policy has helped preserve Russian rights while the existence of Russia has aided American policy in Europe and in Asia.

The vital, and least appreciated, phase of our practical world policy has been our attempt to support the British Empire and to share in its destinies and in its profits. No policy could be less popular in either the United States or in the Empire. Two proud, stubborn and pugnacious peoples are involved, not counting the Irish—two nations which have done each other dirt and profited by each other's difficulties, turn and turn about, for a hundred and fifty years. Yet when the historian of the future unravels the secret history of this present age, of the financial co-operation, double-crossing and skullduggery, of the oil and debt and naval squabbles, of the Bank of England and Federal Reserve operations, of the decline of sterling and the attack on our gold reserves, of the British and American and Dominion tariffs, he can only conclude that here is no ordinary antipathy. Deeper than the instinct to profit at each other's expense, is the American desire to rescue and to control, financially, the British Empire; equally deep is the corresponding British desire to isolate and to control, politically, the United States of America. On the British side are generations of skilled statesmanship, prestige and a world-wide empire; on our side is the simple fact that we contain the bulk of the wealth and of the population of the English-speaking world. Where the Communist, the Nationalist and the Internationalist see two groups of Anglo-Saxons fighting each other, the realist sees two groups, each trying to preserve and to control the other's resources.

Hence the real international issue of 1932 is not German reparations or European disarmament, not Russian propaganda or peace in Manchuria. The real problem is whether the British of the United Kingdom can throw into the scales against America the British of the Dominions, circumscribe our influence and cripple our trade with the Empire, and thus force us into the British line-up in world affairs. From the American point of view, the question is whether we can maintain our new-found independence of British capital and British trade and then attract into our own orbit the British Dominions which share our language and our political heritage. There is no war to the death; it is almost a love affair. It is peace in its most virile and intimate form. On the solution of this issue depend the Americanization of the British Empire and the partnership of the United States, as an unofficial Dominion, in the British Commonwealth of Nations.

You can't dramatize a fact like that in an American election. Whether we are to inherit the British Empire, as we inherited the Spanish Empire, is too big a question to be discussed in American party politics. Neither side dare avow, if it even recognizes, its motives. Tariffs and loans, dollars and sterling, ships and films and bills of lading and lecturers and propagandists, these are the counters in this unique and unsuspected struggle between the nation of shopkeepers and the nation of salesmen to determine which shall be the senior partner in the coming economic merger of the Anglo-Saxon race. Logical Latins, dogmatic Communists, will not understand what is happening. Prophecies of war and of alliances will be cooked up on the theory that the British and Americans are, of economic necessity, destined to be enemies. Our own idealists and alarmists will see in this fact a grave menace to peace and all sorts of wild statements will be made by college professors. But Latins, alarmists, idealists and Communists will deceive themselves if they imagine that this rivalry will lead to bloodshed. In any crisis, America and the Empire will stand together against the world, no matter how much they may hate doing so.

Under such conditions, our policy of peace—loudly proclaimed and diligently sought after in every diplomatic cupboard and under every political sofa—is the best policy we could possibly follow. We aren't going to fight for world power because we don't need to fight for it. It's headed in our direction. At the same time, we must let others see that we are pure in heart, so that it will be difficult for our rivals to label us as a military or naval menace, as Germany was labeled in the years of her rise to power. We must also see that our powers of defense are strong enough, so that only a big coalition could beat us. As coalitions are formed by fear, rather than greed, so long as we prattle about the beauties of disarmament and continue to watch our step, none of the great powers will fear us, though they may all despise us. World contempt is a high price to pay for world peace but it is not prohibitive, if it leads to world power.

Whether world power will be a satisfactory substitute for American prosperity is difficult to determine. As the strain of hard times continues, it will be hard to resist the temptation to take short cuts to what we want. As we feel the pressure of the unofficial British boycott of American goods, we may be driven to violence or to compromise. As the full weight of the British propaganda against Americans and American civilization spreads through the Empire, through Europe, through South America, through Asia and even into Russia, we may be betrayed into foolish explanations or childish bitterness. We may, if goaded sufficiently, be tempted to strike out at some small and offensive nation, in an attempt to expand our trade or our influence, and so be tricked into a new spasm of "imperialism" which will definitely put us back into second place. But if we grin and bear it, keep our heads and our tempers, the British may be the first to weaken, and then we will discover that we dominate the economic life of the greatest political organization in human history.

The election of 1932 will not make much difference to the final outcome of this struggle to win the peace of the twentieth century. If the Republicans are beaten it means that the party pledged to economic nationalism has been displaced, but it will be at the cost of direct American participation in world politics. The Democrats of 1932 are political nationalists and this fact will hamper any inclination towards economic internationalism. The great danger of a Democratic Administration is that it may start a fresh series of interventions and imperialistic adventures in the Caribbean and in South America, which would play into the hands of our rivals for the trade of the American republics. If the Republicans win, they will maintain the tariff and financial system which is slowly giving us the mastery, despite colossal blunders and losses, but their policy of co-operation with the League of Nations, which is the symbol of their readiness to compromise with European politics, will also be maintained. This means that much of what the Republicans gain through economic Sinn Feinism will be lost through diplomatic inexperience. Either way, the process will go on and on until we are ready to make our final decision as to whether we shall control or be controlled by the British Empire.

The war gave us power and the peace is giving us education. Except where power and intelligence are linked, you have chaos. What we need from the modern world is a peace which will give us time, time to learn, time to develop the brains with which to use our resources to our best advantage. Hence we are all for peace, peace at any price which does not include the subordination of our power to the will of others or the abdication of our intelligence. We are finding it difficult to obtain peace on these terms, for if we do not know what it is all about, other nations do. That is why peace is an important issue in our politics, but we can't say so in any terms which make sense to any man who can see behind the headlines.

XII

Home and Mother

IF HERBERT HOOVER had not been orphaned at an
early age, he could not have made the promotion of
home-owning the central feature of his policy. Only a
man who had an unhappy childhood could be so deeply
interested in the welfare of the child, and only a man
who had lost his childhood home could believe so
strongly that our national salvation lies in the home.
Underneath the statesman, the politician, the engineer
and successful business man, we see a sad and frightened
little boy whose parents died in Iowa, leaving him to be
brought up by relatives in the Far West. Here we see
the Hoover who has never grown up and who is trying,
as all of us try, to recapture a lost golden age and hoping,
as few of us dare hope, to leave it as the monument to
his memory.

The legacy of the orphan is the real object of Hoover's
policy and it is destined to become, secretly or openly, an
issue in his campaign for re-election in 1932. It would be
amusing if it were not so human. America—the land of
the skyscraper, of the apartment house and of industry
on skids—to become a nation of homes in the third dec-

ade of this century! Within a fortnight of the date on which he addressed the home-owning conference in Washington and almost on the very day on which he recommended that Congress establish a system of Federal Home Loan Banks to finance home-building, several thousand homes in the District of Columbia were advertised for sale to recover taxes due to a District Government in which the residents of Washington have no voice. There is the answer to the own-your-own-home movement in 1932. We are, in fact, a migratory people, nomadic as were the Indians we displaced, restless and changeable; few of us hope to spend our lives in the same place where we were born or where we began in business; we are constantly on the move, by choice, by necessity, by prosperity, by depression. For most of us it is better business and far safer to rent than to buy and for most of us just now the problem is to keep the homes we have, even though they are rented, rather than to settle down for ever and ever and acquire a house on the installment plan. If the government need do anything about homes, let it attack the inflated values of real estate and the scandalously high costs of construction. The application of the economies of mass production to housing and the deflation of the real-estate racket would do more to stimulate home-owning than a billion dollars of federal credit. But to attack building costs is to attack the entrenched power of the labor unions and to deflate real estate is to threaten the solvency of our

banks; and so sound politics, as well as emotion, decree
that there shall be no fundamental reform of the rent
and mortgage system which is the underlying cause of
the high cost of living and of loving.

So with child health. No one could more genuinely
approve of childhood than does the President. The dis-
graceful infant mortality in this country is a national
dishonor. The women who die in childbirth alone make
a mournful regiment in the blood-stained advance of
our very cheerful and oh! so scientific civilization.
When Bryan Untiedt of Colorado rescued his school-
mates in a blizzard, he was invited to the White House,
but those who thought that the President was playing
cheap politics with the courage of a simple boy were
cruelly mistaken in their estimate of the man. They
should not forget that in his campaign he vigorously
refused to "kiss babies for publication" and stuck to his
refusal. He simply believes in children, deeply and un-
affectedly, and signalizes his belief at every opportunity. Yet the devil of doubt inquires whether child welfare and child health might not be better served by
vigorous advocacy of a Constitutional Amendment
prohibiting child labor than by impressive conferences
at Washington. One wonders whether such gestures as
the reduction of medical costs, which, much to his credit,
is being promoted by Secretary Wilbur through the In-
terior Department, are not mere maneuvers and whether
a real reform in the distribution of the national income

would not be more effective. But that, we know, is communism and hence intolerable to a free community.

However, Home and Mother are destined to be good vote-getters in this election. In any country where song-writers make fortunes out of the simple word "Mammy," where motherhood is an institution, an obsession and a mania, and where the Home is regarded as the citadel of all virtues and the summit of human happiness, loudly to praise the home is good politics. Plucking at the heart-strings is an ancient electioneering device, and can any candidate be blamed for hoping that the women will vote for the man who publicly praises the domestic hearth in preference to the man who prattles about tariffs and kilowatt hours? It is good politics and, better still, it is sincere politics. Hoover's attempt to solve the problems of the twentieth century by leading a retreat to the nineteenth-century home would be a political master-stroke in any year but this.

As a means of applying automatic lungs to our paralyzed prosperity it is hard to beat. Certainly home-building is a more intelligent use of our surplus wealth than was the purchase of beautifully engraved foreign bonds and brightly colored stock certificates during the Mellon market. If the billions lost in the foreign bond racket and on margin had been applied to the development of American real estate and housing, this country could have been converted into a garden in the decade after the war. As it is, our homes—such as they are: mortgaged, flimsy and tax-ridden—are the foundation of our economic life. An orgy of home-construction would restore prosperity for a time and would do far less damage to the country than a new industrial boom. The mortgage bankers, the contractors and the building unions; the lumber, brick, cement and quarry industries; the makers of bath tubs, kitchen stoves, furnaces, hot-water heaters, window glass, wire screens, shingles, gutters, and furniture; the installment salesmen with their sewing machines, washing machines, electric refrigerators, vacuum cleaners, automobiles and radios; the gas, water, telephone and electric utilities; insurance companies—fire, theft, life, accident and bonding—all would benefit from a big revival of building. An enormous stimulus would be given to consumption and the capital hitherto wastefully and destructively devoted to financing industrial production far beyond the purchasing-powers of the public would be rendered not only harmless but really useful. Far worse remedies for the depression have been proposed than Hoover's plan to encourage home-owning.

Again, the American home is the crushing answer to the spread of communism. A nation of home-owners, especially if the homes are being acquired by "easy payments," is not going to do anything radical to the business system which supports them or to the government which protects them. A nation of property-owners and taxpayers is not going to have patience with any theory which attacks private property or increases taxes. Every man shall sit beneath his own vine and fig tree, we shall cultivate our own garden, and the ugly social ideas begotten by industrial feudalism in the prolific womb of European slums will perish in the bright light cast by the twinkling hearth-fires of the American nation. The home is the solution of the paradox of capitalism: its determined wastefulness, its duplication of effort and multiplicity of services create demands almost as extravagant as those of war and offer a solution to the problem of over-production. Home-owning is, in fact, the bourgeois ideal of society—the vision of a happy nation and a healthy people as the chief object of policy—as it is also the Christian ideal of society—the ideal of a system based on individuals linked in durable marriages, monogamous and co-operative rather than a promiscuous and collective mass, a herd or army, as envisioned by the hard-eyed apostles of Karl Marx. It is finally, the democratic ideal—the creation of a group of voters, each with his stake in the country and each on an equality with his neighbor. The scheme is, intellectually, a perfect solution of all our troubles.

There is only one flaw in this bright dream—it is not true of modern life, and of all vain efforts, the effort to restore the past—whether the past be that of the Romanovs of 1917, the Bourbons of 1789 or the Iowa homestead of 1880—is the supreme folly of statesmanship. The unequal distribution of American wealth dooms the home-owning movement in advance. Worse still, the instability of American wealth would destroy such homes as were constructed.

Wage cuts, business failures, passing of dividends, default of bonds, bankruptcies, unemployment, replacement of human energy by machinery and of animal energy by oil and electricity, are not only producing a situation in which only one-tenth of our people enjoy reasonable comfort but are creating an environment in which even that tenth is constantly shifting. The great enemy of the American Home is not Bolshevism, not the automobile or the films, nor even atheism or birth-control: it is industrialism. Industries migrate from one part of the country to another in quest of cheap labor or cheap power; industries merge and industries perish; sometimes they leave the country altogether in search of raw materials or better markets. Industry reaches into the home for the labor of women and children and uses it to beat down the wages of men. When an industrial worker marries he is henceforth at the mercy of his industrial boss. He has to take wage cuts lying down and if, in addition to a wife, he has acquired a home, he is doubly the prisoner of the payroll. As a result, the age of marriage rises and the birth rate drops and our moralists strain at the gnat of contraception and swallow the camel of an industrial system which encourages celibacy in the masses.

So, too, is capitalism the enemy of the society which

created it and which it has in turn created. Where every man has to fend for himself, the incentive to saving is enormous. The individual *must* prepare for the rainy day by buying life insurance, putting his money in a savings bank or on deposit, even if he doesn't try to make a quick fortune by buying those "sound industrial stocks" which have been hitting new bottoms for over two years. Whatever he does, his money goes back into production, more and more production, which is just what we don't need, and is withdrawn from consumption, when consumption is precisely what we *do* need to keep our economic system from corkscrewing society into insanity. Between them, industry and capital have created a system which is reshaping society, draining people from the countryside into the industrial centers and then subjecting them to permanent insecurity, taking them out of homes and crowding them into apartments, tenements or hovels and then making them produce more goods than they can afford to buy. A program of federally financed home-building on the Hoover Plan—more and more and moratorium—is powerless to withstand this gigantic and tyrannical impulse of our age.

Nevertheless, in his advocacy of the home and his preoccupation with childhood, President Hoover has stumbled upon the greatest issue of our times. Unfortunately, it cannot be solved by a political election any more than a vote of the League of Nations could affect the Einstein

Theory, or the decision of the Vatican against Galileo could halt the march of science. We are all—Soviet and Capitalist alike—in the grip of terrible and uncontrollable forces. We have created a business system which is stronger than we are. New processes and new inventions, new needs and new discoveries, are destroying human society—including the American Home—as we know it, yet cannot tell us what we are to receive in its place. While we know that the mass of people will keep right on living, marrying, begetting and dying, we shrink from the changes into which we are being thrust. A vote for Hoover and the Home or for Curtis and Child Health won't make a particle of difference to the final result.

As a temporary system of inflation to tide us over the depression for a few years, the use of federal funds to finance a pyramid of mortgage bonds is a very practical idea. Even after the mortgages are foreclosed and the industries which have been stimulated are closed down again, the houses will remain and will offer shelter to people in the future. In the meantime, Home and Mother provide suitable soft music for an election which will be fought with every weapon known to God or man. The women's vote may thereby be lured into the Republican camp, although it is possible that our politicians exaggerate a girl's eagerness for a home and children of her own—when put into political slogans it somehow suggests the rabbit hutch or the studfarm. It is also possible that, with millions in real distress and thousands of homes being sold for taxes within rifle-shot of the White House, American women may regard the public yearnings of the President for a nation of homes as being either sinister or silly.

However, silliness never hurt a candidate's chances, provided he be sincere, and Hoover is sincere in this. Since he lost his childhood home he has been a rolling stone. Just now he lives at 1700 Pennsylvania Avenue but he knows that he won't be there forever. Like all those who have been uprooted, he craves stability and seeks it by turning back to the only stability he ever knew, back to West Branch, Iowa, twenty years before McKinley. His is the old, the traditional American ideal, his is a policy of economic antique-hunting. It is a pity that this policy and this ideal come exactly fifty years too late to save America from her growing pains as a world power in the twentieth century after Christ, but they will be worth a lot of votes, for all that.

XIII

Farm Relief

TEN million votes await the man who tells the American Farmer that he is the salt of the earth, the backbone of the nation, and the chief object of political agitation. Fifteen million votes await the man who has the nerve to tell the American Farmer to go to hell. If there was ever an individual who has been inflated monstrously out of proportion to his real importance it is the man with the hoe who has been flattered by the politician with the hokum. The farmers have been howling for help since the dawn of the Republic—for the government to drive the inconvenient Indians off their lands, for cheap farms, for free farms, for railroads, for low railroad rates, for money, for free silver, for irrigation, for cheap fertilizer, for a tariff on farm products, for the export debenture, for the equalization fee, for Farm Relief.

The farmer has arrogated to himself all virtue and all knowledge, he has planted prohibition in our vitals, he has voted against progress, against civilization, against the city, against science, against art. He has made and unmade Presidents in the image of Main

Street, he has exhausted our soil as he will exhaust our Treasury if given half a chance. He is the great obstacle to human progress, the great threat to political stability. Sooner or later, we shall discover—as the Roman Church discovered, as England discovered, as Soviet Russia discovered—that the pagan, the landed proprietor, the kulak, is simply so much mud on the path of progress and must be swept aside if society is to advance.

These are harsh words but they are justified. The American Farmer as a political institution is a danger to our civilization. It was the Farmer who condemned Stopes for teaching evolution in Tennessee. It is the Farmer who lynches the Negroes every time the price of cotton slips under the deadline. It is the Farmer who dominates the politics of a dozen prairie states and periodically raids the rest of the nation for his personal profit. There is nothing wrong with agriculture as a career and lots of worthy people are habitually engaged in farming, but the Farmer—that social scarecrow in whose name our major political crimes are committed—is another matter. He constitutes a politically self-conscious and aggressively self-satisfied minority which holds the balance of power between the two great parties. Accordingly, he has been flattered and cajoled until he really believes that he is the whole United States and that no city dweller is a real American. In a score of states, democratic government and fair representation have been rendered a farce by the Farmer's insistence on retaining control of government through obsolete and unrepresentative Constitutions. For a decade, the Farmer refused to re-apportion congressional representation, as required by the Constitution, because it would give the cities more power. Just at present, the crime of the century—Prohibition—is being kept in force simply because the Farmer blocks its repeal. The Farmer is a bad winner and rotten loser and deserves about as much sympathy as any other man who feels that it is the government's duty to pay him for being kind enough to exist.

Sooner or later, some party will discover that the country is fed up with the Farmer and will turn him loose, like the rest of us, to fend for himself. In 1932, however, both parties will be bent on seducing the farm vote and will be only too glad to send the bill for the doped gumdrops and the agrarian aphrodisiacs to the taxpayers of the East. The horny-handed sons of the soil will be sitting pretty in a year when the Democrats hope to invade the prairies and when the Republicans will make any sacrifice—at other people's expense—to keep the Farmer an honest woman.

Under these circumstances, the Farmer will discover that he needs relief as never before. And he will be right, but no one will have the courage to say that it is his own fault. He has dug his own grave and shoveled the dirt on his own face by persistent and extravagant over-production. His is the catastrophe of bumper crops.

Every large country in the world is now competing with our wheat farmer: Canada, Russia, Australia, the Argentine, South Africa are all producing wheat for export and, despite the Farm Board's purchase of 200,000,000 bushels of American grain, wheat has been selling at the lowest price in fifty years. Too much wheat for too little money is what ails the Farm Belt. One might pity the grower if he had not been repeatedly warned to cut his acreage, diversify his crop, and restrict his output. A specialist in giving moral and political advice to others, he did not have the brains to accept the advice of those agencies—the Farm Board and the Department of Agriculture—which had his welfare at heart.

The same thing has happened to cotton as to wheat. Russia, India, Nigeria and the Sudan are growing more cotton and people are wearing fewer clothes. Other textiles—silk, rayon and woolen—are growing in popularity, but the cotton farmer refused to heed the sign of the times or the advice of his betters. As a result he produced over 17,000,000 bales in 1931, unloaded seven million of them on the banks and the government, and still saw the price drop to less than six cents a pound. He refused to destroy a third of the standing crop to give economic value to the remainder, as suggested by the Farm Board.

When Huey Long of Louisiana and the cotton-minded statesmen of the South tried to pledge him to take a holiday in 1932, he balked. Half of the normal crop will be planted in 1932, according to present plans, but anyone

who believes that the cotton farmer or the wheat farmer
or any other kind of farmer will keep his word, if he
sees a chance to get ahead of his neighbor, is a candidate
for Congress.

It simply is not in the farmer to practice birth control
on his crops, in the face of the Divine Command to increase and multiply. He artlessly believes that the other
fellow will keep his word in crop-restriction, but he
reckons that he himself will take advantage of the situation and so plants more and more. As a result, he has
achieved the distinction of forcing America back to
economic barbarism, to the substitution of barter for
commerce. When the Farm Board swapped wheat for
Brazilian coffee, the whole world turned back to the
Dark Ages.

The farmer's folly is going even farther than that.
So supremely smug and self-satisfied is he with himself
as an institution that he refuses to face any form of
competition which is not based on his own methods. The
future of agricultural production lies with the machine,
the big farm, the application of industrial methods to
agriculture. Thomas Campbell of Montana has shown
that it can be done profitably in this country. The Ca-
nadians, Russians and Argentines have shown that it
can be done elsewhere. But the spirit of Kansas—the
spirit which gave us the Civil War and the Eighteenth
Amendment—says no! "There ain't no sech animule." A
movement is growing to prohibit big farms just as laws

are being framed to prohibit chain stores. Nothing must be allowed, says the farmer, which will make me less important or which will demonstrate my inefficiency. So he sets up a moral yammer against Russian competition, he sets up an unconscionable tariff against Canadian competition, he sets up legal barriers against the competition of the American industrial farm, and then has the gall to go to Congress, a vote in one hand and a collection box in the other, to demand that he be paid for the privilege of remaining inefficient.

He will not come away empty-handed in 1932. The most conservative estimate is that it will cost the country half a billion dollars to bribe the farm vote for the Presidential election. The farmer got half a billion in 1929, through the Farm Board, for what was humorously known as "Farm Relief." In 1932, he will demand at least as large a sum in cash and will go much further.

He will demand, and he will get, a higher tariff on food, so as to put the city dweller at his mercy. He will demand the equalization fee, by means of which the American consumer will pay a high price for food in order that the farmer can sell his food to foreigners at less than cost. If denied this privilege, he will demand the export debenture, by which he will be paid to export his produce and allowed to collect by means of a tariff rebate, to the disadvantage of the Treasury, of the consumer, and of the industrial producer. There is absolutely no limit to what the farmer will demand, as of divine right, from the politicians who fawn on him for votes.

The consequence will be fatal to the farmer and disastrous to the country. Encouraged, by federal subsidies, to maintain a volume of farm production in excess of the demand for his goods, the farmer will go broke by townships, counties and whole states. He will bankrupt every political organization which is foolish enough to try to save him on his own terms. He will be evicted from his homesteads by tens of thousands, rather than adapt himself to a new state of affairs. He will ruin every bank which lends him money; even the Federal Land Banks will be paralysed by his insatiable demands for credit, while the local banks will close their doors by the hundred. And finally, after ghastly losses, inhuman suffering and violent political upheaval, the farmer will wake up and find that he has become socialized along with the rest of us.

That is to say, he will discover that he is a part, not the whole, of society; that his views on foreign policy, public finance, art, science, the city, hydro-electric power, war and peace, alcoholic beverages and the relation of the sexes, are interesting but unimportant; that the government owes him no duty, no help, no money, which is not due to every other member of society; and that co-ordination and co-operation, rather than anarchy and greed, is the alternative to rural individualism. Sooner or later, the American Farmer will find his salvation by working with, rather than grafting on, the rest of the nation. He will discover that industrial farming, collective agriculture, co-operative marketing, when combined with control of production, specialization and elimination of poor lands, will offer him his best chance to make a self-respecting living.

The 1932 election, however, won't teach him this necessary lesson. We are only beginning to talk of industrial planning, after fifty years of conflict—strikes, panics, booms, failures and reckless competition. It will take the Farmer at least twenty more years of hard luck to realize the need for change. He is like the proverbial Yankee who started his ploughing with the reins tied around his waist. The team ran away and, as the poor man remarked afterwards, "Before I had been drug forty rods I seen ,my mistake." The only effect of this election will be to determine which party shall get the credit for bribing the farm vote. If the Democrats win, they will concentrate on helping the cotton farmer of the South and the wheat farmer in those states which vote for the Democratic candidate. The Republican farmers of the Far West and of the East need expect no help, be they ever so miserable. If the Republicans win, they will keep right on taking money away from the East and shipping it out to Borah-land, in order to help the virtuous Wheat and Corn Belt get higher prices from the East for the West's noble produce. The fruit-growers and vineyardists of California will be helped—

is not the President from Palo Alto?—and the cotton-growers will get what is left. Either way will be very expensive and will only prolong the farmer's agony at the prospect of change.

For that is the central fact of the Farm Relief problem. The farmer refuses to change with the times. No one wants him to go bankrupt, to be evicted or to join the wretched set of landless croppers. At the same time, no one wants to submit to the Kansas idea, that because a man gets his living from hoeing corn and cotton, cultivating wheat, herding sheep and cattle, or tending fruit trees, he is thereby rendered so holy, wise and infallible that it is the duty of the rest of us to accept his views on what to drink, whom to elect, how to run the country, and in return to pay him handsomely for being a failure at his own job. Work is a painful necessity for most of us, a pleasure and an opportunity for a very few, but no sort of work is superior or inferior to any other sort of work and least of all does agricultural work endow a man with moral or political superiority.

In the case of farming, work seems to produce a stubborn and dangerous opposition to change of any sort, religious, moral and political. The world moves, just the same, and the farmer is moved with it. It is a crime that we should be required to spend a billion dollars to make it possible for the farmer to postpone his understanding of this very simple fact. For his temporary success means that some day, some leader or some party will be compelled to rouse the people against the farmer and crush him as an obstacle to the national welfare, as he has been crushed in every nation and age which has experienced his predominance. The fact that it is good politics now to help the farmer is going to make it better politics in the future to injure him. It is a shame that he cannot be changed by less drastic methods, but he has taken to politics and the problem of Farm Relief will become, not how shall we relieve the Farmer, but who shall relieve us of the Farmer?

XIV

Bribes for Buddies

THERE are about four million veterans of the World War in this country and they all have votes. With their families they constitute just about one-tenth of the population of the United States and are just reaching the most active stage of their lives and careers. It is practically impossible to keep them out of politics and, as a matter of fact, they are in politics to stay, or until the next war. About a million of them are organized into two nation-wide gangs—the American Legion and the Veterans of Foreign Wars—and they have already cost the government over five and a half billion dollars —more than enough to give us the finest navy afloat and the best-equipped professional army on the planet— through the Veterans' Bureau, and will cost us three or four billion dollars more through the bonus. By the time they get through, they will have nicked the Federal Treasury for a sum running between sixteen to thirty-two billions, if they live up to the record established by their predecessors in the art of trading veterans' votes for pensions, the Grand Army of the Republic. And not one Congressman in twenty has the courage to stand up and say "No!" to the ex-service men who have already cost the taxpayers more than we have spent on all the veterans of all our other foreign wars put together.

The veterans' racket is utterly shameless and without any legal basis which can be distinguished from black-mail. It is unpopular to say so, but there is no more rea-son why an able-bodied veteran should be paid a bonus by the government than that any other citizen should be able to cash in at the Treasury as the price of his citizen-ship. To prevent the repetition of the outrageous pension system which flourished after the Civil War, the govern-ment established compulsory insurance for its armed forces during the World War. Those who were wounded or injured in the course of their service are clearly en-titled to the best care which we can give them and are, in fact, being cared for. Those who died in the line of duty have had provision made for their dependents through the insurance system. The rest, for having done their duty, are entitled to nothing. Let's put this straight! Those who enlisted voluntarily took their risk with open eyes; those who were caught in the draft had no choice in the matter; both of them deserve nothing but the moral credit which is due to disciplined courage and self-sacrifice in the service of their country. Such sentiments undoubtedly seem treasonable to the profes-sional veterans, the "buddies" who gang the Treasury whenever the public payroll looks as though it would yield to a line-plunge. They even go so far as to imply that no one not a veteran has any right to criticize their claims or to have a voice in the costly policies which they recommend to the country for the benefit of their own pockets.

By the same token, only the farmers would have the right to determine the amount of money spent for, and the character of, farm relief; only the unemployed could decide whether and what doles should be paid them; only the income-tax payers should determine the amount of their income taxes, and so on. Such is the creed of anarchy and plunder, and so long as the veterans' organizations support it they classify themselves with the political prostitutes who keep Washington supplied with its noisome army of civic streetwalkers. Could there be any greater absurdity than the spectacle of organizations which contain a total of a million members deciding what shall be paid to them by the other 124,000,000 Americans for a military service which was largely involuntary, often devoid of danger, and entirely a part of the basic duties of citizenship? What could be more subversive to the national safety than the spectacle of the organizations which profess to support national defense, raiding the Treasury of the funds which could secure that defense?

Wherever they can slip a political tentacle or a financial siphon into the national cash register they have done so. Veterans must receive preference in Civil Service examinations. Why? Merely because they want an unfair advantage over their fellow citizens. Veterans must receive preference in unemployment measures, for the same reason. Veterans must be compensated for contracting ailments which are discreditable to themselves or which were not incurred in the line of duty. The insurance system for veterans is rapidly being broken down. The Legion advances on the Treasury, as the Germans were accused of advancing in Belgium, behind a screen of women and children. Bills are being introduced which propose that widows of veterans who died of injuries not incurred in the service shall receive pensions. They call this putting the widows of World War veterans "on an equality" with the widows of veterans of the Civil and the Spanish Wars. It is proposed that veterans shall receive free medical attention in government hospitals for injuries and illnesses incurred in civil life, and that the year after which a veteran's marriage shall not entitle his widow to an annuity shall be pushed forward from 1932 to 1941. Inasmuch as we are still paying pensions to the widows of veterans in the War of 1812, this is no idle threat. It is proposed that the Senate, like the House, shall establish a special Committee on Veterans' Affairs, so as to give the ex-service lobby a foothold in the upper chamber of our government.

What do the veterans want? Money! They showed that in the "bonus" grab of 1924. They then demanded what they called "adjusted service compensation," an attempt to conceal the fact that they were looting the government by describing what each veteran received as the difference between the pay he got from the army and the high wages he might possibly have earned in industry if he hadn't been in the army. By 1931, under this law, there were nearly 3,500,000 "adjusted service" certificates outstanding, with a face value of three and a half billion dollars, payable in the 1940's, while almost 130,000 more veterans had walked off from the Treasury with cash in their pockets. In 1931, with a falling revenue and rising demands for relief of unemployment, the veterans rushed the Treasury again. All decency and legality was swept away, Congress, as usual, played dead dog, and the veterans got the law changed so that they could borrow from the government up to 50% of the face value of their certificates. As a result, over a billion dollars went blooey in the worst year the Treasury had had since the war. Coolidge vetoed the bonus grab in 1924, Hoover vetoed it in 1931, but the Congress knuckled under and passed the bills over the Presidential vetoes. As the representative of the American Legion told the Ways and Means Committee, with unblushing effrontery, the Legion had resolved that to pay cash at once to the veterans "would be an appropriate demonstration of the gratitude of the nation to those who carried its arms in 1917-18." The man who spoke for the equally avaricious Veterans of Foreign Wars was refreshingly frank: he simply reported that the National Encampment of his outfit had gone on record "as favoring the immediate payment of these adjusted compensation certificates in cash."

The stage is being set for another big bonus grab before the election of 1932. Like everyone else, the veterans need money this year, and, despite their good resolutions, they are going to press for—or their vote-snatching Congressmen are going to propose—the immediate cash payment of the full face value of these certificates: a sum which works out at around $2,-300,000,000. The politicians this year will need every vote they can beg, borrow or steal and they will pass the buck to Hoover without pity or remorse. Neither party will take a chance on losing the allegiance of the veterans—the race will be too close; neither of the veterans' organizations will take a chance on the other's getting the jump on the bonus. It required a special trip by President Hoover to address the Legion Convention at Detroit to stave off a bonus vote in 1931, but the Veterans of Foreign Wars did not miss a trick. *They* came out boldly for the whole hog. To hell with the Treasury, to hell with the taxpayer, to hell with national credit, to hell with the country! Give the Buddies cash!

The mischief of this situation is that it fits in pretty neatly with the plans of some of our far-sighted and less scrupulous statesmen. To them the bonus is the least of several evils. It is, first and foremost, an effective substitute for the "dole." With nearly four million veterans distributed according to the general population, it is one way of putting money in circulation where it will do most good. With so much money being shipped West to help the farmers, the bonus is one of the few means available to the Eastern taxpayer who wishes to keep his money at home. Moreover, pensions are an effective counterirritant for socialism. In the first place, they serve to subsidize the militantly and loudly patriotic groups who would resist any real social reform. In the second place, the veterans will gobble up all the loose cash in sight and will exhaust much of the credit which might be used to finance social reforms by the government. Finally, the veterans play directly into the hands of their archfoes, the pacifists, who see and state clearly that the demands of the veterans must cut down the expenditure on national defense and also bring patriotism—whether real or professional—into nation-wide disrepute.

The joke of it all is that our "veterans" saw the least fighting and suffered the fewest hardships of any major army which engaged in the World War. Not more than half of them got overseas, and not more than half of those saw front-line service. In the two years of hostilities they suffered fewer deaths and injuries than are inflicted by our automobiles in two years of peace. Our troops fought well on the Western Front, but they did not fight long or hard, as compared to the troops of England, France, Germany, Austria-Hungary, Russia,

Italy, Belgium or Serbia. For comparison you have to go to Japan, Greece and Rumania. Such fighting as we did is entirely to our credit, but it was nothing which justifies our pensioning every member of the A. E. F., let alone the troops who never left this country, for the rest of their natural lives. The Old Gray Mare did not perform so nobly on the Western Front that we are justified in giving her a permanent stall in the Mint.

It is probable that this consideration is responsible for the fact that three-quarters of the veterans—who are, after all, average, decent citizens when not inflated by martial memories—have nothing to do with the professional veterans' organizations, and that very substantial minorities in those organizations strongly oppose the "gimme" spirit. At both the Boston Convention in 1930 and the Detroit Convention in 1931, the Legion voted down the bonus. In the first instance, the "gimme" gang stampeded the Legion's executive committee into overruling the action of the convention. These organizations are primarily social and patriotic, and are composed of genial small-town "joiners" who haven't an ounce of malice in them, but they are being used for political or financial profit by a minority of their members, much as the Ku Klux Klan was used by its Imperial Wizards and Kleagles back in the days of Coolidge. The Legion contains about 900,000 members, the Veterans of Foreign Wars owns to 125,000, and the Disabled American Veterans have an enrollment of 30,000. Of the three, the last is most deserving of public sympathy, the V. F. W. restricts its membership to those who saw active overseas service, while the Legion is the catch-all outfit. Hence the Legion is becoming primarily political, while the V. F. W. is primarily professional. Both, however, conform to the general trend of American organization, in that they are devices which encourage a few ambitious individuals to speak in the name of a huge class of citizens, without warrant of authority or fear of reproof. (The Federation of Women's Clubs and the W. C. T. U. use precisely the same tactics.) To hold their membership, they must produce results and so they are forced, by their own political necessities, to demand that pensions be paid by the government to the veterans, as a special and superior class of American citizens.

Pensions have been a very costly business to the government, and being based on no useful form of economic service, are extremely depressing to the taxpayer. Up to the beginning of 1917, the government had spent over $5,200,000,000 on soldiers' pensions, of which all but $300,000,000 had been extorted by the million and a quarter Union veterans of the Civil War—an average of $4,000 per Union soldier. We have already spent close to $2,000 in relief and bonus on each of our 4,057,101 service men in the World War, on the average, and if the ex-service men run true to form we are due to spend from $2,000 to $6,000 more apiece before the country wearies of their exactions. At the end of 1930, we were still paying pensions to widows of the War of 1812 and the war with Mexico, to over 200,000 soldiers and widows of the Civil War and to an equal number of soldiers and widows of the war with Spain. These are not war widows, except in rare cases, but the widows of veterans, many of whom married long after the war was over. If the four million "veterans" of the World War are not checked in time we shall still be paying pensions on their account in the year 2050 A.D. The only question which confronts us at this moment is, how soon are we going to begin paying general pensions to World War veterans, chucking aside all the elaborate and expensive arrangements which we made in 1917 to prevent that possibility from arising? The best guess is that the veterans will have got the full face value of their adjusted "service" certificates by 1933 and that in 1934 they will win the drive for "liberalizing" various features of the present system, so as to clear the decks for a real raid on the Treasury in 1936. When the country is paying over a billion dollars a year on military pensions to men who saw a minimum of war service, in addition to the half-billion now spent on hospitalization and insurance, we shall begin to discover the real meaning of taxes.

The veterans won't be an issue in the 1932 campaign —worse luck!—as the efforts of politicians of both parties to win their support or to anticipate their wishes will be decisive in keeping the question "out of politics." The great majority of veterans who live their lives, raise their families and pay their taxes will be ignored, and a few noisy politicians and those greedy misfits who figure that it isn't stealing to rob the government, will render fear of the veterans the beginning of wisdom for Presidents and for the Treasury officials who must find the funds to keep them happy. Slowly but surely, the veterans will grow in pride, in power and in disrepute until—as happened with the Grand Army of the Republic—their leaders will overstep themselves and the public will lose patience with the glory-grabbers and flag-flappers who regard a few months in khaki as a permanent meal ticket.

This will not happen in 1932. No politician in this election will dare tell the truth to or about the veterans —they're organized. True, the organized veteran vote couldn't be delivered and wouldn't pay much attention to any politician, but the politicians don't know that. And besides it wouldn't look patriotic to appear to question the divine right of the American Legion to sound the Mess Call in the Mint. So the veterans' vote will be bought and paid for, but won't be delivered, and the country—including the veterans and their own families—will have to foot the bill for a colossal and useless attempt to bribe a good-sized chunk of the electorate into good-natured approval of peanut politicians. Nothing else would be "good politics," as not one politician, and not one Presidential candidate, has the courage to realize that by putting the veterans in their place today, the country can be saved a future outlay as great as our present national debt. Some day the man who smashes the veterans' racket will get the winning votes, but that won't be until 1940, at the earliest.

XV

America First!

ETWEEN the Hoover Moratorium in June and the
meeting of Congress in December, 1931, a new
issue appeared in American politics. For the first time
since the Republicans won that "great and solemn referendum" in 1920, which wrecked Wilson's policy and
broke Wilson's heart, American nationalism and the idea
of American isolation from the "wicked" Old World
has reared itself as a practical issue in a national election.
It had taken ten years of careful and intelligent effort
on the part of the Republicans to live down the 1920
campaign and to drive the American electorate to the
point at which they were about to drink the waters of
internationalism. Slowly, step by step, we had moved
into active co-operation with the League of Nations, co-
insurance of world peace and promotion of international
disarmament. Then, at the eleventh hour, the raucous
cry of "America First!" was raised and the American
people prepared to shoot the works as far as Europe was
concerned.

As usual, the outburst took everyone, including the
Administration, by surprise and, also as usual, it served

as a warning to our statesmen not to underestimate American patriotism, and to foreigners, not to overestimate American generosity. The Congressional debates on the moratorium were conducted in terms of grassroots sentiment and proved beyond the slightest doubt that the fundamental mood of the American people is just as anti-foreign as when Henry Cabot Lodge blocked American ratification of the Treaty of Versailles. Every government in the world—including the American Government—has been warned that the Americans are not willing to commit any more noble gestures, in the name of world peace or European recovery. Instead, the people of this country are quite ready, for the time being, to let Europe and Asia go hang. This single fact has completely altered the political situation, almost overnight; it has put a bomb under both parties and it has touched off explosive passions which may determine the outcome of the election.

The immediate causes of this sudden swing towards "America First!" are so simple and so obvious that only an internationalist could fail to see them. In the first place, the Hoover Moratorium did not bring back Prosperity by the return mail and did not even settle the European problem. When it appeared that its net result would be to make our taxes high by a quarter of a billion dollars, in the midst of hard times and a Treasury deficit of two billions, the universal suspicion arose that the real object of the moratorium had been to help Europe at our expense. More important still was the complete and scandalous breakdown of the pretensions of the League of Nations in the face of the Japanese aggression in Manchuria. We were pained to discover that, in spite of the fact that we sat officially with the League Council, the Japanese went right ahead with the military invasion and administrative alienation of the territory of a fellow member of the League. Having been assured for years that the war debts were the cause of most of Europe's troubles and that our absence at Geneva crippled the League's peace-making machinery, it would have been a miracle if we had not concluded that the whole debt and League propaganda had been hysterical and unreal, and that the Europeans were simply trying to put over a fast one.

Less definite but even more fundamental a cause of our outbreak of nationalism was the realization that hard times in America were partly caused by hard times in Europe. We resented the consequences of our economic interdependence with the rest of the world when it appeared that this interdependence put our banks at the mercy of Hitlerism in Germany and our farmers at the mercy of the purchasing power of the English pound. Our instinctive reaction was to pull the covers over our head and pretend that the footsteps we heard creeping along the hall were not burglars but mice. And finally, a large part of American nationalism was simply party politics, an element of the wave of anti-Hooverism which was sweeping the country like a vacuum cleaner. If Hoover was for the moratorium, that was reason enough for many people to oppose it. If Hoover wanted international co-operation, hurrah for isolation! The natural impulse to heave a brick at the foreigner became a release mechanism for the political desire to heave a brick at Hoover. His foreign policy became a symbol of the man in office and a scapegoat for his unpopularity. All of these forces reinforced each other and stiffened the nationalistic opposition to war-debt reduction and every other form of diplomatic charity to the deserving poor. What! With millions out of work at home, make a present of $240,000,000 cash to the Europeans? It was a pushover for the Irreconcilables.

Back of these immediate causes, "America First!" sentiment reflected other forces which were more general and which were world-wide in their character. The entire world was going through a nervous crisis of nationalism and it would have been a miracle had we escaped. Nationalistic governments were in power in every one of the British Dominions. India was seething with nationalistic sedition and in Great Britain a nationalistic government had just received the largest majority in British political history. In Germany, the Nationalists, led by Hitler, were demanding power on a platform which called for the end of reparations and the revision of the Treaty of Versailles. France, under the influence of Tardieu and Poincaré, was using her

money, her diplomacy and her armaments to advance
her narrow national interests, without caring a row of
czarist roubles for the effect on other nations. Italy was
still under its violently nationalistic Fascist dictatorship.
Even Soviet Russia, the cradle of the Communist International, had adopted in the Five-Year Plan a policy
which, so far as concerned its effect on the outside world,
was indistinguishable from the most virulent form of
economic nationalism. And in Japan, after ten years of
patience, the imperial army had thrown off all restraint
and had gobbled up Manchuria, despite the existence of
several perfectly beautiful scraps of paper designed to
prevent exactly the sort of thing which the Japanese
army had accomplished.

The world-wide tariff war and the world-wide scram-
ble for gold, with its financial double-crossing, its banking skullduggery and its "raids" on the pound, the
mark, the yen and the dollar, emphasized that this is
still a world in which Morgan helps only those who
help themselves. And finally, there was a wave of general boredom with American idealism. There had been
too much talk about our "duty" to Europe, of Europe's
"duty" to disarm, of France's "duty" to forego reparations, of "the new Japan"; too much explaining away
of the Monroe Doctrine, too many diplomatic attempts
to castrate British and American naval power, too many
pacts and projects and protocols, and not nearly enough
emphasis on the selfish practical values of world co-opera-

tion. We had never been told what we would get out of it, always what we must give; never what it was worth, always what it would cost. That ignorance of and prejudice against every other nation, which exists everywhere and is nowhere stronger than in the Mississippi Valley, finally succeeded in the turning, not of the other cheek, but of the worm. We had had enough. As a result, we approach the 1932 election in a mood of complete boredom with the rest of mankind. We are bored with the League, with the World Court, with the war debts, with disarmament and with reparations. We are bored with Japan, Manchuria, the Nine-Power Treaty and the Kellogg Pact. We are bored with international bankers, foreign bonds and domestic idealists, and we would like to forget the whole kit and kaboodle and mind our own business for a time.

Since we do not yet realize it, we shall have to be taught by experience that internationalism is a necessity in the modern world. Every nation is a part of every other nation, when rain in the Argentine can help the Dakota wheat farmer and when the political ideas of a German agitator can shake the credit of American banks. We can take our choice between the sort of internationalism which is diplomatic and co-operative and that which is socialistic and revolutionary. What we have not yet realized is that the alternative to international co-operation is no longer spread-eagle nationalism, but is world revolution, and that an attempt to act on

168

the basis of "America First!" is bound to turn into the cry of "All Power to the Soviets!"

However, this will not keep nationalism out of the Presidential campaign. What we shall experience is an attack against both kinds of internationalism in an effort to capitalize our instinct for isolation into votes. The Republicans will attack radicalism and will attempt to coin anti-communism into ballots for Herbert Hoover. So long as the war debts were not involved, this maneuver had all the elements of a winning issue in a country which is heart and soul dedicated to a non-communistic catch-as-catch-can philosophy of life. Unhappily for Hoover, the moratorium gave the Democrats a chance to start an anti-European war dance and to sound the alarm on debt cancellation. Hoover was "exposed" as a man who would give Europe a quarter of a billion dollars and who still refused a dole to the unemployed. As the newsies chanted after the President saw the leaders of the Non-Communist Hunger Marchers: "All that Hoover gives the unemployed is sympathy. Big-hearted Herbie! He gives till it hurts!" The resentment against hard times was short-circuited against Hoover's far-sighted policy of forebearance and co-operation with that portion of the world which is our best market and our most important political rival. The American people saw red and the Democrats, with dawning joy, realized that Hoover had put a deadly weapon in their hands. Chagrined to be caught on the unpopular side of a patriotic prejudice for the first time in their party's history, the Republican leaders tumbled over each other to get on the nationalistic—and anti-Hoover—side of the war-debt question. The moratorium was passed in a form which practically paralyzed the administration's foreign policy at the beginning of the most critical year in contemporary history.

If the moratorium had brought back prosperity before the autumn, Hoover would have been hailed as the greatest statesman in modern times; as it is, it seems simply to have angered Europe and to have given the Democrats a winning issue. It is one of the most bitter ironies in our history that the party which was defeated in 1920 because it supported American membership in the League of Nations should receive its first chance to return to office twelve years later because the Republicans had been trying to work with Europe and with the League to restore prosperity and maintain peace. The joke of it is that, in 1919, the Democrats tried to head off anti-Wilson sentiment by letting Mitchell Palmer, Wilson's Attorney-General, start a vicious anti-radical crusade, and were swamped in a wave of Republican nationalism. In 1932, if the Republicans try to outguess the electorate by taking a crack at the minions of Moscow, they run the risk of being submerged in a new wave of Democratic nationalism. The Democratic case is a strong one: the Republicans have scrapped the splendid navy which Wilson was building, they have proposed to reduce the war debts which Wilson refused to cancel, they have let the bankers link our fortunes with Europe, without giving us, as Wilson proposed to give us, a *quid pro quo*. This situation contains all the elements of a Democratic victory and, wise or foolish, it will commit whichever party wins the election to a policy of caution and nationalistic reserve in dealing with the rest of the world for the next few years.

Its immediate effects will be deplorable. The co-operative idea in world politics will be given a black eye. Political hatred based on money—the most vicious and unreasonable of all hatreds—will rage unchecked over the debt and reparations question. As the fires of patriotism mount higher in every country, disarmament will become less than a pious hope and will prove the graveyard of diplomatic reputations. As the capitalistic world is convulsed with controversy over the age-long question of "Who pays who and why?" and as the disarmament pledges of the Treaty of Versailles and years of work by the League of Nations are junked, the capitalistic mode of life will be discredited. In its place, the system of revolutionary communism will receive encouragement and the world will have presented a magnificent opportunity to Moscow. So far as we are concerned, our first tendency will be to adopt a hard-boiled nothing-for-nothing type of foreign policy, to regard the French as a set of shortchangers and to insult the British with proposals to trade their possessions for the money they owe us. We shall find ourselves isolated, for not even the Germans and Italians, who now look to us for sympathy and support, will stand up for us if France and England are united in a common hatred of our desire to be repaid our loans. We are in for a big dose of international hatred and a dangerous dose of international isolation, which will remind us that we are the wealthiest, the most hated and worst defended of the great powers of the world.

Hence "America First!" is apt to prove a boomerang to the party which adopts it. It will, however, demonstrate to other nations, and to ourselves, the need for international co-operation. Patriotism is no longer enough, not even as a refuge for the scoundrel. Pure nationalism no longer works in a world which is slowly becoming a unit. We—and every-other nation which is today indulging in a nationalistic orgy—will be taught that our choice lies between the two types of internationalism: Wilson's and Lenin's.

We shall also be taught that world co-operation depends on a fair consideration for the rights and interests of others. We shall learn to respect the national policies of other nations and, by adopting a nationalistic policy ourselves, shall teach other nations that our assistance cannot be obtained so long as our rights and interests are ignored. After the campaign of 1932, the world will have a more accurate, if less flattering, idea of our international outlook and will learn not to take us for granted. In the meantime, a little nationalism will give us a breathing spell and a much needed chance to solve some of our own problems, without worrying about the gold reserve of Patagonia or the problem of Kamchatka. It will put a damper on those people who get more excited about the difficulties of the German Reichsbank than over a thousand bank failures in the Middle West and who work up more moral indignation over the size of the French army than over the reign of legalized terror in the Kentucky coal fields. It will do us and the world no harm if we take a little time out from world-saving and set our own affairs in order. It will also do Europe no harm if we assume that the Europeans are capable of solving their own problems without our political meddling. It will be a very good thing indeed if this wave of world-wide nationalism encourages every nation to mind its own business a little more and interfere with its neighbors a little less. A period of homely self-determination, untainted by idealism, will do us all a world of good and may make possible in the future the sort of co-operation in which foreign countries recognize that we intend to stand up for our rights and our interests and in which we realize that our diplomats are not literally inspired by the Holy Ghost whenever they get outside the twelve-mile limit.

So the injection of nationalism into the election won't do us much permanent harm and will do the Democrats a lot of good. After all, it is an old American custom to go back and touch first base whenever a foul ball is called, and there is no sense in denying that internationalism of the idealists, by the government, for the bankers, has gone very sour. If we dig up what George Washington said about foreign entanglements, it may cause a lot of trouble and embarrassment, but sooner or later we shall be taught that we are not the only frog in the puddle, while Europe will realize that it is useless to expect diplomatic miracles from the United States. It is all part of our political education to learn that patriotism is no substitute for intelligence and that internationalism is not a policy but a necessity in the twentieth century. It is part of the world's political education to learn that internationalism in practice must be based upon the nations which exist today and that idealism is no substitute for national loyalties.

Granted that the surge of nationalism in the United States is strong enough to swamp the Republicans, and granted that Hoover has put his party so far into the internationalist camp that it cannot retreat, just as the Republicans learned after 1920, so will the Democrats learn after 1932 that world co-operation is the condition for the survival of civilization as we know it. So the election may produce a lot of red fire and loud yells of "America First!" from the isolationists; the tub-thumpers may brand Hoover as a friend of every country but his own and broadcast the inaccurate and unflattering theory that our diplomats are incapable of looking out for themselves every time a wicked European catches them at Geneva, but when the winner is in office he will quickly discover that we must keep on working with other nations or let Moscow run the show. Nationalism may prove to be the winning issue, but that is all it will be, and if it is, it will only show that American elections are won on the most convenient, rather than the most important, issue of the day.

XVI

Doles, Debt and Taxes

W HEN the heat and tumult of the campaign has
passed and the country has been saved from a
fate worse than death, when one man or another has been
elected President and the Democrats or the Republicans
have triumphed, we shall discover that there has been
very little real change and that nothing much has happened. The old problems will survive under new forms,
the old jobs will be held by new men, and the practical
results of the election of "A" or of "B" will be just about
like twins. America will learn, as other nations have
learned, that there is a limit to what can be accomplished
by political action short of revolution; that people will
be born, fed and clothed, will grow up, marry and die,
whether we have anybody or nobody in the White
House. The real life of the people will keep right on and
society will have to meet its problems, irrespective of
politics.

Among the things which are going to happen to us,
after the election, are the dole, the increase in the public
debt and the stiffening of taxation. There's no sense de-
ceiving ourselves on these points. We already have the

dole—only we find it smells much sweeter by some other name: charity, the bonus, appropriations for public works, drought relief, farm relief, utilization of the Farm Board's wheat for feeding the unemployed, the National Credit Corporation, aid for railroads and land banks, cheaper credit, state and city emergency appropriations, Community Chests, Strike Funds, Red Cross drives, part-time employment, and so on. We have the dole today, in the sense that every solvent American is compelled by charity and taxation to contribute directly and indirectly to the support of unemployed labor and unemployed capital.

The public debt is rising for the first time since the war. We began by using the war-debt payments for current expenses. We continued, in the face of falling revenues, to pile up the congressional appropriations. We had to borrow to meet the Treasury deficit in 1931; in 1932, faced with a two-billion-dollar deficit, we proposed to abandon the sinking fund. With fresh demands for a soldiers' bonus, for more farm relief, for unemployment relief, for "economic reconstruction," the pressure for further borrowing will inevitably bring higher debts. Higher debts mean higher taxes. Secretary Mellon proposed to restore the high income-tax rates of 1924, to apply luxury and amusement taxes, and taxes on bank cheques. The government employees are being compelled to surrender three days' pay for unemployment relief, are being denied the promotions to which they are entitled under the law, and are threatened with salary cuts. In order that the government's credit may be good for the necessary borrowings, the government must repudiate its obligations to those who work for it and must tax its citizens more severely. That is elemental and neither Republican nor Democrat can escape the logic of the situation.

The easiest thing, of course, is to borrow, but who will lend, except upon onerous terms, to a government which lacks the courage to apply the necessary taxation to its people? The old-line sources of revenue are not sufficient to pay the government's bills. We are in for an era of bigger deficits and higher taxes. The deficit was a billion dollars in 1931, two billion dollars in 1932, and will be two or three billions in 1933. Whoever is President on March 4, 1933, will discover that the public debt has risen five or six billion dollars since the congressional elections in 1930. The world-wide trade depression has cut the ground from under the Treasury, while the raids on the mint are exhausting the national credit. We are in the position of a man who is working on part-time, who can't meet his rent, and whose wife must have an expensive operation. The Smoot-Hawley Tariff Act of 1930 has helped kill the customs revenue—its rates are so high that two-thirds of our imports are on the Free List; in other words, it is an efficiently protective tariff. The national income has dropped a third, as a result of the depression, and has knocked the income-tax receipts for a row of decimal points. Only the tobacco tax has held up. Our people were never in a worse state to stand more taxation and they must be taxed. Borrowing was never more difficult, and the government must borrow.

To borrow means that the government offers the rich a secure investment of their present wealth, at the expense of the next generation—which is perhaps why some of our very wealthiest men have suddenly been smitten with lust for a "Prosperity Loan." Increased taxation transfers part of the expense to this generation and, by our ideal system of graduated income taxes, forces the rich to become richer, at the expense of the poor, in order to pay their surtaxes. Either way, the bulk of the nation must pay the piper and, as we shall have to try both methods, we shall pay both now and in the hereafter.

This situation is slowly educating us to the need of a complete overhauling of our quaint olde tyme tax system. It is ridiculous and contemptible that the government of the wealthiest nation on earth should have to tremble before the voters and the bankers in order to meet its running expenses, when huge areas of taxable wealth are allowed to lie idle. The existence of tax-exempt bonds is a challenge to organized government in the United States. The fact that states, counties and municipalities can issue bonds, the income from which cannot be taxed by Washington, is an unhealthy situation, leading to wasteful local borrowing and to the hoarding of wealth in unproductive investments. The liquor traffic, as it exists today, if subjected to the pre-prohibition excise tax, would net the Government close to a billion dollars a year, a sum which now goes to graft, crime and the financing of lawlessness. A high sales tax on luxuries and a low sales tax on staple necessities would give the government direct access to the ocean of day-by-day commerce. A small flat-rate income tax of 1% collected at the source on all payrolls, salary checks, payment for services, dividends, bond coupons, rents and royalties, would remove the element of uncertainty, evasion and perjury from the present income-tax system, while that useful measure could be retained as a surtax pure and simple. The existence of our post-office system suggests that a graduated stamp tax on bills and cheques—two cents per hundred dollars or less—would be easy to collect, while first class mail could pay higher rates. The free list is a scandal to the customs administration. We should apply what is known as a primage duty of 5% of the value of all imports, over and above the existing rates of duty, and thereby get revenue as well as protection out of the tariff. We might even consider subjecting interstate commerce to an annual license fee for individuals and corporations, on a graduated scale, and reach after the nine-tenths of our commercial life which is not covered by foreign trade. Until the government makes up its mind to tax the real wealth of this country in its effort to balance the books, our finances will remain on an airy and fastastic basis and the people will have to pay dearly for every shift in the economic winds and every miscalculation at Washington.

As it is, the government has broken so many pledges —or blasted so many expectations—that its credit is at a low ebb. We were given to understand that we should have tax reduction and now we are faced with increased taxation. The war debts, which were pledged to debt retirement, were first used to pay current expenses and were then remitted by the moratorium. The sinking-fund operations—though prescribed by law—have been compromised and the Treasury itself, in its fatal series of blundering admissions, talked itself out of a promised surplus and into a billion-dollar deficit in the spring of 1931. Until Secretary Mellon submitted his drastic report to Congress in December, 1931, there was no sign that the Treasury admitted that taxes were going up and that public credit was going down. With the Democrats in control of the tax-levying lower house, it was possibly good politics to make that admission, but it was also good sense.

By the time the election is over, the American people will find that the following results have been accomplished: There will be a higher income tax and surtax levied on about ten per cent of those who are in receipt of taxable income, about four million out of the forty million people who are "gainfully employed." The rich will pay very high taxes and will turn around and, un-officially, collect from the poor from five to ten times the amount which they pay in at Washington. There will be a sales tax on luxuries but not on necessities. There will be no tax on beer, because such a tax will not be legally possible with the Supreme Court dedicated to the theory that the Eighteenth Amendment must be "liberally construed." The national debt will be much higher, national credit will be much lower and government bonds will be at a considerable discount.

Anyone who thinks that the election will alter this situation is walking in his sleep. Will the election reduce the national debt, with every politically organized group in the country clamoring for cash? Will the election reduce the national expenditure, with the greater portion of our budget—debt service, veterans' relief, post office, defense and administration—practically outside the power of government to modify and still live up to its obligations? Will the election increase the national wealth or the national income? How? The only matter which might be decided by the election is whether the government will improve its tax system. To do so implies a basic change in our tariff policy and hence a tariff revision. Can you see either party doing that after the last tariff mess? It implies the elimination of tax-free bonds and the legalization of alcoholic beverages—both of which require a constitutional amendment and both of which are, accordingly, not within the powers of

Washington. It implies a drastic overhauling of our income-tax system and a multiplication of direct taxes which will advertise to the voters the heavy costs of pre-war methods of government in a post-war world. And can you imagine either party increasing the number of conscious and indignant taxpayers from four to forty millions?

Whether "A" or "B" enters the White House, whether Republicans or Democrats deal out the jobs and the contracts at Washington, you will find that you have to face a period of difficult national finance, that your taxes will be higher and your income lower, and that all the time the government will be running up debts in your name while you are compelled to pay the "doles" which are appropriate to the illness of a badly demoralized economic system. There's no use voting for anybody under the impression that your taxes will be lighter or that the government will be run along intelligent financial lines: the taxes will be high and the government won't change its spots, and no President can do a thing about it.

XVII

Soft Money for Hard Times

ANOTHER matter which will not be affected in the
slightest by the outcome of the election is the
problem of money. After a golden age of thirty-five
years, the whole world is headed back to William Jen-
nings Bryan and his peculiar idea that money is not a
thing itself, but is an agent of society, that man should
be the master of money, not money the master of man.
The British Empire, with the exception of South Africa,
had gone off the gold standard by the end of 1931. In
Europe, only France, with the second largest gold reserve in the world, could be regarded as likely to maintain gold money. Japan had gone, South American
countries had gone, and Soviet Russia had never been
on the gold basis. In America, while it is inconceivable
that the government would willingly abandon the gold
basis of our currency so long as the national debt must
be redeemed in gold, it is certain that hard times will
compel the government to promote softer money for
the convenience of the people who depend on money
for the maintenance of life. The movement towards a
silver standard of money was checked in Bryan's day by

the discovery of huge amounts of gold in South Africa and the Klondike. In our times, we shall have to find "gold" in our own brains if we are to soften the blow of economic disaster.

It is important to remember that gold money is only a token, like wampum, adopted as a convenience for the exchange of goods and services. You can take money into a shop and trade it for a beefsteak or you can use it to hire a man to mow your lawn. On the other hand, if you want to trade a load of hay for a barrel of flour, a month's telephone bill, five gallons of gasoline and a pair of overalls, or if you want to exchange your own mental and physical skill and energy, for board and lodging, entertainment, food and clothing, you get money for what you have and give it for what you want. For convenience's sake, gold—the one metal which does not rust and which is so rare that a small quantity of it can safely be used to represent a great value—has been generally used for money. In modern society, this gold is generally stored in banks, while larger numbers of slips of paper, representing the gold, are used instead. These notes, in turn, are used to create credit and thus our entire business civilization is reared in a large pyramid of paper debts, based on a smaller amount of paper money which in turn rests on a limited amount of gold. Every time a small sum of gold is withdrawn from the base of that pyramid, a larger sum of paper money must be retired, and a much larger amount of credit is destroyed. Gold can be withdrawn from circulation, in this way, either by transfer to another country or by private hoarding, which creates an artificial scarcity of gold. At the present time, gold is being hoarded everywhere.

"Abandonment of the gold standard" by a government means that it refuses to trade its own paper money for its own gold, on demand, and prefers to keep the gold in its vaults than to maintain its credit in international and national transactions. This means that the paper money of that government loses its value and that prices rise. In national trade, the process is called inflation; in international trade, it is called depreciation. When a government maintains the gold system, and reduces credit and currency in proportion to its loss of gold, the process brings lower prices and is called deflation, in national trade, and the maintenance of the sanctity of contracts, in international trade.

Our present problem is one of deflation. Gold, being scarce, has risen in price and therefore the price of everything else has gone down. Wages have fallen; wheat, oil, cotton, coal and every other form of wealth can buy less money than before. This means that anyone who owes money is out of luck, if he borrowed before the crash. Our entire civilization is on margin. Debts contracted when wages were high must be paid when wages are being cut. Mortgages placed when cotton brought eighteen cents a pound and wheat a dollar a bushel must be paid with cotton worth five cents a

187

pound and wheat bringing fifty cents a bushel. Deflation puts the entire debtor class, on about 99% of our people, in the power of the creditor class. This would be grand for the creditors if it were not for the fact that they want to be repaid. They can't be repaid unless the debtors can lay their hands on the money, and with everybody scrambling for that money and with that money scarcer than a kind word for Hoover, it is easy to see that the creditors are out of luck, too.

Hence the general demand for inflation, from debtors and creditors alike. Hence the rush back to Bryanism, the eagerness to devise some system which will make money more plentiful, easier to capture and less expensive to domesticate. The demand for inflation has become irresistible and the effect is to push the government into a soft-money policy which is bigger than politics and which will take effect irrespective of the election of Whoozis and the triumph of the principle of Whatnot. People have a stubborn habit of surviving the blunders of both governments and business systems, and they are certainly not going to be such fools as to perish in mass simply because the money system has blown out a couple of fuses. Restoration of prosperity by money is the only alternative to the reorganization of business by revolution, and is, accordingly, the great political issue of our day. The problem of restoring "prosperity" is simply to put more money into circulation, without destroying the value of that money, to inflate credit, without inflating currency. In other words, we've got to find a way of making our money soft without making it soggy, or else we've got to stand aside and let the socialists shoot the works.

Nobody knows just how to soften money. A large group of people, particularly those who produce silver, claim that we should base our paper money on silver as well as gold. They point out that there's a lot of silver in the world, that half the human race uses silver money, and that by adopting two metals instead of one you can increase the amount of money without having it run wild. Also, as we control the bulk of the world's silver production and own the bulk of the world's gold, we couldn't lose. Another method is that which we used quite successfully during the Civil War: to have the government sell bonds which can be redeemed in paper money rather than in gold and to authorize the banks which purchase them to issue their own bank notes against the security of these bonds. This is inflation pure and simple, but can be kept under control by the government. The principal objection to this idea comes from the present bondholders, who are entitled to be repaid in gold, and who want the government's credit to be maintained. A third way is for the government to borrow huge sums of money on its own credit and to distribute this money to the public in the form of pensions, doles and public works. This is the quickest and the most expensive form of inflation. Finally, there is the indirect system of inflation already adopted by the Hoover Administration, under the alibi of "economic reconstruction," in using national legislation, political influence and federal funds to release large amounts of bad debts and frozen assets (i.e., loans which cannot be repaid and securities which cannot be profitably sold) through the National Credit Corporation, the Federal Land Banks, the proposed Home Loan Banks, the revived Finance Reconstruction Corporation, the new banking legislation, and the new "anti-hoarding" bond issue—a deliberate increase in the public debt disguised as a measure to restore idle money to circulation. This latter system has the advantage that it uses a small amount of government credit to create a large amount of commercial credit, and hence does not destroy the value of money, merely starts it moving again.

The real question, however, is whether the release of bad debts and the construction of public works is enough to help the mass of Americans. Our basic difficulty is that, in creating our high-tension industrial system, we have been short-circuiting our people out of the economic hook-up. We have enabled a smaller number of men, with a larger amount of machinery, to monopolize the business of production and exchange. The rest of us are not really needed, but we have got to eat just the same and we are going to insist on working out some new way of wangling wampum which will enable us to get what we need. For the first time in human history, the business of producing wealth has become relatively independent of labor, and the money system, which once gave labor the wages with which to buy what it needed, no longer really reaches a very important proportion of our population. The solution of this problem, short of communism, is not easy. The best brains of our generation will be run ragged to discover a sensible substitute for money as a remedy for hard times.

Moreover, our own problem is only a part of the world problem. International capitalism has broken down. The Bank of International Settlements, which was the international bankers' pet baby, had croup, colic and whooping cough before it had been in existence two years. Tariffs block the free trading of goods; governmental hoarding of gold through the "abandonment of the gold standard" blocks the free movement of capital; defaults, repudiation and cancellation on a Bolshevistic scale by the leading capitalistic powers paralyze the extension of international credit; inflated currencies have demoralized and depressed the world's price structure; and the threat of political upheaval—war or revolution—makes a bad risk out of the most gilt-edged of investments. In Germany, the reparations question has destroyed Germany's national credit and has exhausted her capacity to pay. Great Britain has not only abandoned the gold standard but is doing her utmost to force all other nations to follow her example. France has been using her gold and credit to serve French politics and to impose

French authority, to the injury of international confidence. Russia's Five-Year Plan, after a promising start, has been hurt by the fall of prices which crippled her capacity to meet the commercial obligations she had contracted in foreign countries. Japan went off gold in order to compete with British trade in India and in China. The United States is faced with the reduction or cancellation of her war loans and the default or repudiation of her fifteen billion dollars' worth of foreign investments. Our international credit system faces the worst moral crisis in modern history since the Thirty Years' War. The world is being forced back to barter in international trade and to bankruptcy in international finance. With every nation wedded, in a polygamous union, with the economics of every other nation, it is easy to see that the United States cannot solve her money problem by herself.

As a consequence, the real problem is being pushed into the future by the policy of inflation. Get the election over and done with! is the principle on which both great parties are working. The Republicans are striving desperately to galvanize the corpse of Coolidge prosperity into spasmodic knee-jerks, so that the voters may believe that the dead do rise again. The Democrats, with less to fear from the political Day of Judgment, are anxious to show the people that the Party of Thomas Jefferson sincerely desires to help them in their difficulties. So both political machines can be counted upon to co-operate quietly in the inflation of credit, on the Hoover model, and to postpone the inflation of money, on the Bryan model, until the next administration. Then, win or lose, each party will set to work to make money more plentiful and more accessible to the mass of the people, by the printing press, by the use of silver, or by some new method not yet devised.

It is easy to see that the inflationists will not decide the election. They stand to win, either way, and will be helped by both parties. Generally speaking, the Republicans incline to the inflation of credit and the Democrats to the cheapening of money, but both parties will be compelled to work in the same direction by the pressure of the public demand for quick relief. Unfortunately, neither party has any cure for the real ailment of our sick money system—the failure of the average man to get enough money to buy the goods produced by our industries and our farms. Hence, the result of political inflation will be merely higher prices rather than higher wages, a higher cost of living rather than a broader distribution of purchasing power. Just at the moment we have very high unemployment, offset by very low prices. The effect of inflation will simply bring higher prices coupled with less unemployment. Soft money will prove no cure for hard times so long as we have divorced humanity from wage-labor, through machinery and scientific production, and have made no sensible arrangements to take the place of wages. There are millions of new people being born into the country every year, thousands are being superannuated every year, and millions are being thrown out of employment by the failure of these and of others to get the work to get the cash to buy the food to get the strength to go to work to get the cash to buy the bread to get the strength to go to work. The solution of *this* problem demands such a revolution in our ways of thinking, as well as in our system of money, that anyone who expects either party to pull the solution out of the President's top hat on March 4, 1933, is talking through it.

As a result of the campaign and of the election, we shall receive cheaper money and higher prices, a small increase in employment and a big increase in the cost of living. For any real discovery of what to use for money in this age of super-power, mechanical farming and automatic machinery, we shall have to wait until we, and the rest of the world—Russia included—learn a lot more sense. We shall be lucky if by 1942 we have a glimmering of an idea of the best substitute for gold in an age of stainless steel and stalled statesmanship.

XVIII

Bolshevik Baiting

UNFORTUNATELY for the cause of political liberalism and social progress in America, we face another "Red Scare" and another epidemic of deportations, imprisonment, espionage and censorship, on account of the political opinions of some of our inhabitants. We are so stubbornly opposed to change of any sort that if Bolshevism did not exist we should have to invent it, as an excuse for resisting reform. For a generation there has been an absolute and infantile paralysis of political and social progress in the United States. The World War gave us the alibi of patriotism for parking all of our real problems in front of the national fire plug, and the lucky discovery of Communism after the war gave us an equally good alibi for refusing to answer the summons of our indignant age. Bolshevism enabled us to brand as blasphemy any real measure of reform. Now, willy-nilly, we are in for a new age of political action, and our standpat politicians and anthropoidal industrialists would be less than human if they did not consider as the enemies of society all unfriendly critics of

the political set-up and of the economic free-for-all in
this country.

So Bolshevik-baiting is going to become once more the
American national sport, as both parties seek either to
justify their opposition to reform or to disinfect their
proposals for business and social reconstruction by stirring denunciations of Communism and by official her-
etic-hunts, imprisonments, or deportations of all those
who desire to substitute a democracy for our republic
or to submit industry to popular control. This movement is bigger and stronger than either party and will
swamp any candidate who stands out against it. It represents the natural reaction of the American people
when faced with the demand for change: to believe that
not our institutions but the critics of those institutions
are immoral, and that those who challenge our beliefs
are either inspired by the Evil One or are subsidized by
Moscow.

Anti-radicalism fits too neatly into the political picture to be ignored. With the popular prejudices aroused
on behalf of the Democratic Party by the issues of prohibition and hard times, anti-communism—the only
home-brewed prejudice whose intoxicating effects we
have not experienced—must be imbibed by the Republicans. The only way left for the Democrats is to come
back at the Republicans on the platform of America
First! and not to defend radicalism but to raise the ante
and attack everything foreign. Whether the Republicans

or the Democrats triumph, the radicals will get it in the neck and the next generation will reap a prickly little crop of political wild oats, in the shape of new Mooney-Billings imprisonments and other Sacco-Vanzetti electrocutions. Both parties will agree on the wickedness of Russia, and, when the votes are counted, there is no doubt that a great number of ballots will be cast against Russian Communists.

The anti-Russian gang is too strong to be pushed aside in 1932. It includes the American wheat farmer who has been taught to blame low grain prices on the "dumping" of Russian wheat on the world market and who dreads the idea of the collective or industrial farm on the Soviet model as a threat to his independence. It includes the American manganese miners and lumbermen who are faced with hopeless competition against the huge undeveloped resources of the Soviet Union. It includes the American labor leaders who resent the Communist efforts to seize control of the unions by boring from within and who have found that, in negotiating with the employers, the fear of Bolshevism is the beginning of high wages. It includes the great moral and numerical strength of the Catholic Church which, under the promptings of the Jesuits, has declared undying hostility to the atheistic and materialistic state created by the followers of Karl Marx and which, though tolerant of political and business relations between Italy and the Soviets, is a unit in opposing such relations between Ameri-

ca and Russia. It includes the professional patriots, the
D.A.R.'s, and the national order of flag-flappers, who are
never happy unless they can find some terrible "menace"
to denounce and to whom Russia, being remote and
hairy, is an ideal whipping boy. Finally, it includes Bab-
bitt—all the small employers of labor and all the petty
businessmen who regard a demand for higher wages, for
shorter hours of work, or for the right to form a union,
as virtual treason to the American Constitution and repudiation of the Ten Commandments.

The overwhelming strength of this anti-Red line-up
dwarfs the petty group which favors radical reform at
home and friendly relations with a government which,
despite its bad manners and its economic naughtiness, is
working damned hard to make life better for the mass
of its people. The biggest bankers and industrialists, who
would have most to fear from a real Communist movement in this country, have shown themselves quite
open-minded and tolerant to the Soviet system, but—
radical propaganda to the contrary notwithstanding—
they have no real political following in this country.
The professors of politics and economics who feel that,
irrespective of governmental disputes, there is a natural
community of interest between Russia and America or
who regard it as absurd that any group of thick-necked
American politicians should feel free to excommunicate
the economic and social practices of another country,
are a pitiful handful who are encouraged to keep their

ideas to themselves. The intelligentsia, who are vaguely disturbed by the ease with which deputy sheriffs and policemen can beat up or kill workers, or who feel that Russia is trying out an experiment which may help us solve our own problems, or who have read a few books on Russia and therefore think they understand it, have no political influence. The pro-Communist group in America would scarcely fill the Yale Bowl, while the Communist Party couldn't even elect a state Assemblyman, so long as the professional politicians count the votes.

This means that, Communists being few, anti-Communism is good politics and that anti-Russianism serves a very practical purpose. Even if we are going to apply radical remedies to the very serious abuses in our civilization, we must do so in terms of American, not Russian, institutions. Our problems are so different to those of Russia that Bolshevik methods would be ridiculous. There would be almost as much sense in borrowing from the Chinese their entire system of government, or in adopting Gandhi's goats and spinning wheels. We are quite right to resist the application of Soviet methods to our institutions. Where we are wrong is in resisting the application of radical ideas to our problems. The secret of the anti-Communist drive is the stubborn hatred of any change or reform at all on the part of the business leaders of America. What they want is not restraint but fresh privileges, not government control but government aid. They are seriously alarmed by the sudden rise of political unrest and social discontent and they cannot conceal the fact that both of these disturbing elements are caused, not by Russian propaganda, but by the failure of our business system to make the grade without going into second gear. They are fighting to stabilize the situation in America as it is, and, lacking the traditional boob-soothing bait of prosperity, they can only throw up a barrier of passion and prejudice against the forces of change.

The stage has been carefully set for this trick and the crafty old men who run the Republican Party have left nothing undone which would interfere with the dramatic entrance of the Bolshevik bogey on the political stage in 1932. The Secretary of Agriculture has told the farmers that Russian wheat sales were a deliberate plot to ruin the American farmer and thus to create a revolution. The Secretary of the Treasury has been charged by the Tariff Act to begin—on the first day of this election year—to exclude from our Customs the products of forced and slave labor, while the lumber interests have been busy collecting evidence which practically proves that Russian political prisoners are compelled by the Soviets to gnaw down trees with their teeth and then to eat the bark. The Secretary of Labor has won the right to exclude from American soil any foreign believers in communism (unless they come here on business), and is working up a system of identity cards which will enable his merry little men to run out of the country any alien who doesn't like the way in which it has been mismanaged. The Department of Commerce has released every autumn a warning that Soviet commercial credit was about to collapse and the Department of State has tolerated a widespread propaganda against the Russian Government.

Congressman Hamilton Fish has been barnstorming the country, investigating radicalism and denouncing Communism, while Matthew Woll, Vice President of the American Federation of Labor, has been smiled upon by the government and the Catholic hierarchy for keeping anti-Bolshevist sentiment alive in labor circles. When, added to this general agitation of the Red Menace, it is considered that there is not the remotest chance of a real or successful Communist revolution in the United States within the next generation, an ideal opportunity exists for the safe persecution of the small and dangerous-minded minority which regards the jailing of radicals as an imperfect solution of our major problems.

When and how the Bolshevik witch hunt will begin is difficult to guess. If the unemployed move along quietly, it may be necessary to start something in the form of reactionary legislation by Congress which will provoke radical protest and enable the conservatives to declare that the country is in danger. On the other hand, the chances are that distress, strikes and riots arising out of the hardships of the winter of 1931-32 will set the stage to the bankers' tastes and that, by the time the party conventions meet to name their Presidential candidates, the country will be enjoying the patriotic thrill of kicking a man—smelly, hairy and probably foreign—when he is down and out.

The consequences of this Bolshevik-baiting will not be so pleasant. Its first effect will be a temporary but quite definite slowing down of the American movement for social betterment. Political liberalism of any effective sort will be viewed, for a time, with more intense suspicion. New "martyrs" in the class war and the development of an ugly class consciousness will be created by the inevitable stupidity and tyranny or arbitrary deportations by Secretary of Labor Doak and arrests for "criminal syndicalism" by petty state officials. Russia and America, which were drawing closer together at the beginning of the Hoover Administration, will be pushed farther apart and prevented from co-operating at the very time when their common interests in European disarmament and Far Eastern peace are most dangerously exposed to the threat of war. Instead of Moscow being encouraged to abandon world revolution as a bad job, our sudden panic over the existence of a little American radicalism (and God knows that our radicalism is justified by damnable abuses) will encourage the Communist International to believe that its efforts are being crowned with success.

However, all of these consequences will be powerless to keep anti-radicalism out of the campaign or to drive the professional witch hunters out of politics. Anti-Communism may ensure the continued control of the Republican Party by the eastern conservatives and the renomination of the highly conservative Mr. Hoover by the Republican Convention. It may even frighten the Democrats into nominating a safe and sane run-of-the-mine conservative for President—an Owen Young or a Governor Ritchie—although that is not likely. It will certainly tempt the Democrats to include a rabid anti-foreign and anti-Bolshevik plank in their party platform, as they cannot afford to be branded as radicals in the first year since 1916 when they have a chance to win a Presidential election.

However, it is by no means certain that a Republican attempt to run Herbert Hoover against Karl Marx would succeed. The Democrats held their own anti-Red campaign in 1919 and 1920, when Wilson's Attorney-General suddenly started raiding and deporting like Doak, and it didn't save the party from a crushing defeat. The astounding rise of American nationalism since the Hoover moratorium and the Democratic pose of being the only party which wouldn't sell out the country to the European debtors and the international bankers would appear to be better Democratic vote-getters than all the frothings at the mouth of the opponents of political reform and the beneficiaries of business chaos. The conservative frenzy will make things bitterly hard for the alien in our midst, who, though he has helped build up the country, is regarded as a sort of political louse without a right in the world when the hundred-per-centers get on the rampage. The Bolshevik-baiters will make it uncomfortable, unprofitable and, if possible, painful, for any American citizen to advocate a real change in our methods of living and letting others live, and they will thus add an ugly footnote to the long history of American political inexperience. But once the election is over and the country has discovered that everything is pretty much the same, we shall quietly lay aside our witch hunting, put the Red Menace in cold storage, and proceed to forget, as quickly as we can, the fact that we had hysterics in public at the discovery of hostile criticism from within our curious country.

XIX

A Decade of Depression

O NE of our silliest ideas is the notion that politics and business can be kept apart. In fact, every business exerts a political influence and every political event affects business. All that we can do is to establish a sort of dual control over the hot-airship of state and trust that the politician and the businessman will work together, if only to save their necks. This means that politics has no decisive control over business and that a political election has no power to improve business conditions, unless and until the government first gets the necessary authority of dictatorship over the nation's business life. Needless to say, this power is never granted except in time of war—and then most unwillingly— while to obtain it in time of peace from a country devoted to business enterprise is impossible without a revolution.

For this reason, there is no cause for the belief that the 1932 election will cure hard times. If hard times are improved it will be because of forces outside of the control of politics or of business. There may be temporary shifts from more to less depression, as when the dentist slackens the speed of his drill on a sensitive tooth, but the fundamental conditions will remain unchanged and will give us a decade of depression until the emergence, about 1938 or 1940, of the new conditions which will produce —not reproduce—that period of satisfactory exchange which we call prosperity.

The depression is only beginning and will continue until the forces which brought it into being have worked their will upon us. It is not a cheerful thought, but as the human race is proverbially willing to do anything rather than think, it is perhaps just as well that we should have our noses rubbed in the economic mess until we realize that our particular type of depression is inexcusably stupid.

There are no forces outside of America which offer us hope of quick recovery. Europe is overequipped with industrial machinery, with uneconomic frontiers and political hatreds, which intensify competition, destroy purchasing power and impair credit. To improve economic conditions in Europe requires the wholesale revision of the Peace Treaties or their wholesale oblivion, neither of which can be achieved without another war or a general revolution. China is drifting deeper into anarchy and chaos, while Japan, with her armies tangled deep in Asia, is beginning to realize that imperialism is a very sticky stuff. Russia is competing with us in raw materials and, by her monopoly of foreign trade, prevents us from using our surplus production to develop her industries in harmony with our own. The Latin-American republics, with few exceptions, have a low purchasing power and a population which seems singularly indifferent to the idea of buying ice boxes, automobiles, and radios on the installment plan. The British Empire suffers from too great a concentration of population in Great Britain, too few people in the Dominions, and too much antiquated equipment and outmoded capital. Nowhere outside of our borders is there any sign of the credit or the purchasing power which—in past crises—enabled the world to weather panics without changing the systems by which panics and prosperity are alike created. The whole world has gone broke at once.

Our own system offers little hope or encouragement for the speedy recovery from depression. We have too much machinery, more than is sufficient to meet the needs of our population. By the same token, we have too many people, or, to put it more accurately, we have more people than are needed to run the machinery for the production of wealth. As a result—with the largest gold supply in the world, a supply which is regarded by other nations as altogether out of proportion to our needs—we have too little money. And finally, we have too few brains. We have not yet grasped the fact that life is a unit and that wealth has no significance apart from the people who produce and consume it. We have allowed our ability to produce things to get ahead of our intelligence in devising ways of distributing those things. We are like the man in Stephen Leacock's story, who, set adrift on a raft which was loaded with food, starved because he had no can opener. Until we can contrive some system which will enable the mass of our people to get what they need, even if their labor is no longer required by the machines which produce what they need, we shall have depression.

For depressions are not "psychological" any more than the pain felt by a baby who has burned its fingers is "psychological." Depressions are the result of very definite causes, some of which are psychological in origin but whose effects are painfully physical. It may be psychology when Baby decides to put her pudgy little fingers in the pretty stock market. From then on, her sensation is distinctly physical. The symptoms of the depression are, as suggested above, practically incurable at the present time. Its causes, in retrospect, call for a psychoanalyst rather than a physician.

The real reason for the depression was bad leadership, both political and business leadership, for generations. The leadership which produced the Great War—for which we are now paying—also produced the Great Panic. We are still, in the fourth decade of the twentieth century, being ruled by a group of men whose ideas and ideals were formed by the horse and buggy era. The underlying cause of this bad leadership, and of the disasters which it produced, was greed—simple, human greed, naked and unashamed. Economists may call it "the profit motive," biologists "the survival instinct," but it is greed nevertheless and is a necessity of a competitive mode of existence which compels every man to fend for himself and provide for his family as though the human race were still face to face with famine. The result of this greed has been a failure to maintain that steady exchange of goods and services by which the human race supports itself. We have been selling more than we have bought for over thirty years and have taken the difference in promissory notes—bonds and investments—drawn on the future. We have applied and maintained policies of excluding foreign wealth and foreign humans who might help produce wealth, and have persuaded ourselves that we were growing rich and powerful in this manner. Every other nation has been doing the same and some have even gone so far as to restrict or forbid the investment of foreign money in their economic life. Russia, Mexico and the British Empire have been archoffenders in this practice, as we have been in tariffs, and as the British and ourselves have been with respect to immigration; the result is chaos, stubbornly defended and praised as the highest object of patriotic statesmanship. At the same time, our anarchistic attitude towards our own people has compelled every man within our borders to put as much as possible of his wealth into the creation of new means for production, through savings deposits, insurance and investment, until he lacks the means to buy what he has helped produce and thus loses both present benefits and future security at one and the same time.

We still lack any scientific remedy for this economic fever, and must rely on the time-honored, blood-letting devices of starvation and revolt, the fashionable chiropractic of charity, or the philosophical method of accepting impoverishment passively, cutting our losses, and trying again.

We are still unwilling to touch what we call the "trade cycle," namely the alternation of prosperity and disaster. We have not yet brought ourselves to realize that any real cure for depression will probably be as painful as the setting of a broken leg and as dangerous as the removal of a cancer. We cannot decide whether gold is more desirable than goods. We cannot muster the courage to admit that, with the number of wage earners in industry decreasing as a result of machinery, high wages are less important than high dividends, and that eventually we shall have to fall back on the dividends almost exclusively, if we are to give our people the money with which to buy. We cannot yet decide whether we shall regard men as being more or less important than money or whether we shall realize that men and money are simply two sides of the same problem. And finally, we have not yet realized that progress is more important than paper, that a new law means less than an old habit, that a good hen-house is better than nine-tenths of the "market-favorites" we were asked to buy when U. S. Steel was selling for 170 and American & Foreign Power looked like a safe skyrocket to the moon of affluence. We have not yet learned that a sound article sold at a fair price is better than a nation-wide radio hook-up to promote the use of some preposterous tooth paste. We are often regarded as crass materialists. We are actually the most impractical and improvident of peoples. We have wasted the savings of a whole generation in accumulating depreciated stocks and bonds, obsolete automobiles and fading radio sets. We could have put the United States on the road to the conquest of poverty, if we had applied to intelligently materialistic ambitions the wealth which we have dissipated on rosy hopes in the last ten years.

In view of this unwillingness to change the ways of thinking which create booms and panics, to conquer the stupidity and circumvent the greed which brought us to this present calamity, our future is clear. Whether Democrat or Republican wins the election, we shall have another bull market and then another panic, followed by an era of business dictatorship or of political socialism which will take the present system by the scruff of the neck and make it walk the crack of comparative soberness.

The next bull market is already on the way. Dollar wheat before the end of 1932 is distinctly possible, in view of the 600,000,000 bushels shortage in production and the somewhat natural desire of the human race to eat fairly regularly. We are, moreover, thoroughly bored with the depression and are prepared to be optimistic at the least excuse. The inflation which has been launched will start prices rising again and, before the end of the year—provided Europe does not go mad dog about the war debts—we should see signs of the return of "Prosperity." But it will not be real prosperity and it will not last: it will not help the coal industry, the railroads, the cotton industry or the automobile industry to recover lost or losing markets. It will not restore the foreign credit on which so much of our export trade depends or stabilize the foreign currencies which determine the purchasing power of our foreign customers. It will not take care of the millions of people who have no direct stake in production and it will not put back into the hands of the suckers all those stock certificates which were lost in the margin calls of the Panic and which might have served as a new type of currency for the purpose of stimulating the consumption of wealth.

However, new money will pour into Wall Street, from the bootleggers, from the boys who want to play doubles or quits with the stock ticker, from foreign banks and individuals who think that they are on to a good thing, from the widows and orphans and bootblacks. A new wave of speculation, widely hailed as the symbol of a permanent Prosperity, will cheer the country on, and for two or three years we shall forget the unemployed and shall kid ourselves into believing that everything will turn out all right if we don't rock the boat or get any wild ideas about business. Then there will be another crash, not so severe as the last one, and we shall begin to realize that we're playing a losing game. Then, either business or the government—whichever beats the other to the draw—will take full command of the situation and by 1939 we may find somebody in control of events who has both the will and the power to see that henceforth we shall conduct our business in a businesslike and intelligent manner.

This situation is so much bigger than politics that it is ridiculous to expect either party to influence it. Each will take credit for the bull market when it comes and each will blame the other for the ensuing disaster. Only an intelligent and radical group, in business and in politics, which studies the situation as it develops and lays its plans for the catastrophe, will be able to help us. That sort of radicalism is so unpopular in good times and so unsatisfactory in hard times, that it is useless to expect it of any group—the Communists included—which exists at present. It will take more than a candidate or a slogan or a good crop to cure depression. The people themselves must suffer until they really demand a change and their leaders must be forced to think of intelligent changes which will help us adjust our institutions to a changing world, if the twentieth century is going to be one of happiness and real prosperity for any considerable portion of the American people.

XX

A Permanent Wave of Unemployment

JUST as the election will not end the depression, so will unemployment continue after November 8, 1932, when the votes are cast, and even after March 4, 1933, when the winner walks into the White House. We are going to have a permanent wave of unemployment, which will outlast the depression and will become the greatest problem of the twentieth century.

In the hundred years' war between men and machinery, the machines have won. They provide a more efficient type of labor than do human beings. They don't eat. They don't go on strike. They don't lose their skill if they are unemployed. They don't marry and have wives who urge them to ask the boss for an increase in salary or children who need new shoes. They don't get tired or drunk, and, best of all, they don't vote. They are crowding men out of jobs, in factory, mine and farm, and have multiplied our productive population until, in terms of mechanical man power, the United States commands the energies of China. Machines are our coolies, our slaves, our serfs and peasants, and, as is always the case, we are owned by our possessions and take our orders from our own servants. We cannot get rid of machinery even if we wish to do so. And when we allow these machines to throw seven million men out of work and to subject the remaining forty-two million workers in America to wage cuts and part-time employment, we are the victims of a conquest just as sure as though we had imported two or three hundred million Asiatic slaves and used them to do our work.

We are far too inefficient to reconquer our civilization from this occupying army of pistons, dynamos, transformers, automatic looms and high-speed lathes. The whole trend of our mechanical system is, moreover, to deprive the mass of humanity of its ownership of the tools of production. In the old days of home industry, every worker owned his own machinery. Now the ownership of machinery has slipped away from us and has fallen into the hands of vague groups of corporations, syndicates, bankers and speculators, who reap the benefits of capital behind the mysterious veil of corporation law, while the rest of us have nothing to sell but our somewhat superfluous labor.

The result is that, when the machines no longer need our labor, we go unemployed by millions and cannot purchase the output of the machinery which other people own. As these others would have paid us wages if it had not been for the machines, they lose their markets and we lose our standards of living, the machinery stops and waits for us to decide what we shall do about it, and everybody loses.

We don't know what to do. Some of us think that their votes can compel the machines to do our bidding. Fools! The machines cannot read the newspapers or obey any laws except the laws of physics which define their functions. We can be as humane as Lincoln and as wise as Solomon, but no Inaugural Address or Act of Congress can compel a combination harvesting machine to do anything except harvest crops and do so more quickly, more efficiently and at less cost than can many men. We have allowed the machinery to short-circuit us out of production and that means that for generations a large and increasing number of people will not be employed. They may develop into a leisure class as did the ancient Romans whose slaves supported them in idleness, or they may drift and starve and suffer as did the English peasantry when the landlords turned the farm lands of England over to the sheep, but the fact remains that more and more of us will do less and less work.

What we are experiencing is something new in human history: it is the wholesale devitalizing of energy. Until a hundred and fifty years ago, we conducted our work mainly by means of men and animals. Now we use coal, oil, gasoline, hydro-electric power, and are on the verge of tapping the energy of the tides and the heat of the sun. This means that all of our institutions and all of our ideas are being changed. When the draught horse, the mule, and the ox yielded to the steam engine and internal combustion motor, when water power rather than muscles beat the iron and tossed the shuttle, when navigation became a matter of turbines and revolutions per minute rather than of favorable winds or galley slaves, human society received a staggering blow. Power began to shift from those who controlled human labor or human thought to those who understood the ways of an induction coil or the proper lubricant for high-speed machinery. For generations we kept pouring this new scientific wine into the old democratic and religious bottles, and acted as though the ownership of a kilowatt hour was no different than the ownership of a pair of Percherons. Now the old bottles have burst and we are painfully discovering that something new must take the place of the system which resulted from the fact that an individual workman played a decisive rôle in industry. Men, along with other animals, are at a discount in the age of super-power. We are economically deflated in an age which demands the inflation of the human element in industrial society.

Nobody has the slightest idea of what new arrangements are needed to elevate the mass of human beings to a position of real importance in the economic system. However, the unemployed will exert an urgent and ungentle pressure which will eventually compel us to do something. We can look forward to an average of at least three million unemployed during the next ten years.

A PERMANENT WAVE OF UNEMPLOYMENT

Even during the Coolidge boom we had an average of a million out of work at all times. We assumed that, in a nation of 120,000,000, this was nothing to worry about. Now we are discovering that unemployment is the torture to which we must submit until, somehow or other, we discover the means of subduing our machinery to the needs of society. So long as one man tramps the streets looking vainly for a livelihood, so long as one woman grows old and hopeless in the struggle with poverty, and so long as one baby cries for food, our civilization is a failure. Americans became highly indignant when they read that a pervert had brutally murdered a little girl in Cleveland. A gigantic man hunt was organized and the police pledged itself never to rest until the culprit was found. During the same week, a woman walked into the Animal Rescue League in Washington, D. C., and asked them to chloroform a sick cat. The "cat" turned out to be her own baby, a few weeks old, for which she had no food. The woman disappeared into the night, with the starving baby; the police made a few efforts to locate her; but there was no man hunt, no nation-wide thrill of indignation. It was taken for granted. Yet the existence of that starving baby was a greater challenge to American civilization than the brutal assault upon a little girl in a Cleveland slum.

We are starting from scratch with this problem—and we have the best chance in the world of solving it. We have a large and fertile country, inhabited by a race which abounds in brains and energy, and we already possess ample means to provide handsomely for all of our people. We have pledged ourselves to no system for their support and can adopt any method which seems to be workable.

It is almost incredible that, with possibly the most critical unemployment problem in the world—critical because it can be solved with the resources which we are known to possess—we should have taken no direct steps to deal with the situation. We do not even know accurately the number of our unemployed. We know the number of our cattle, of our automobiles, of our houses, of our horse power, but we do not know how many men and women are out of work and deprived of economic hope in this optimistic land. We have no temporary, let alone permanent, way of feeding or supporting those who are in need, aside from haphazard and partial charity. No political party and no outstanding candidate or statesman has any program which promises to take care of their needs. Local levies, charity drives, Red Cross campaigns and emergency measures all aim at relief, but the relief is temporary where the problem is permanent; charity is expensive and it is achieved at the cost of the consumer rather than of the productive agencies which have produced the crisis. And now charity itself is beginning to run dry. For the first time in twenty years, the New York *Times'* annual campaign to raise funds for "The Hundred Neediest Cases" has failed to exceed the sum raised in the preceding year. The Washington Community Chest achieved its quota only by a Presidential order which had the effect of compelling federal employees to surrender three days' pay for unemployment relief. The national income has been reduced by at least one-third and the average man, hard pressed to make both ends meet, is beginning to feel that, with our unequalled productive power, to attempt widespread relief at the expense of the consumer is like pouring water down a rat hole. We are heading for a charity strike which will compel our leaders to achieve relief of unemployment by direct action.

We all know what the result will be. Our present leaders, who still think in terms of horses rather than of horse power and of ownership rather than of use, will try to return to pre-war methods. Their first step will be to ignore the fact of machinery and to assume that wages are too high. There will be, as there have already been, extensive wage cuts, salary reductions, to correspond with passed dividends and defaulted bonds. This pathetic gesture will greatly reduce the purchasing power of the public at the same time that it slightly reduces the costs of production. It will lead nowhere and will produce nothing but resentment.

The resentment will take the form of strikes, lockouts, and riots, offset by repression, police violence and, in extreme cases, martial law. We are in for a decade of industrial violence coupled with unemployment. We shall find that violence is no solution of the problem, that you can't mine coal with bayonets or forge steel with police batons, and we shall strive to end violence and repression by establishing some form of dole or unemployment insurance which will compel the consumers to pay for the human wastage and criminal stupidity of reckless production. This in turn will lead to the revolt of the taxpayers and their refusal to foot the bills run up by our high-pressure industrialists.

That will bring us face to face with the ugly choice which we hate to admit awaits us: we shall have to choose between the gigantic physical wastage of war— which alone is sufficiently prodigal to put our productive machinery to work at full capacity—and the gigantic social wastage of revolution.

Such, at any rate, is the prospect which we shall face so long as old men and old ideas control our actions. When the old men pass and the post-war men take command, neither war nor revolution will be inevitable if we can think in terms of the present and the future, instead of the past. Unemployment is one of the forces which will compel us to think, to think hard and to think clearly. A decade of unemployment will educate our people, and through them our leaders, as to the real meaning of men and machines. The shift from unemployment to leisure and the subjection of the machine to the men whom it serves must be slow and painful, but they are possible.

A PERMANENT WAVE OF UNEMPLOYMENT

Neither political party is now in a position to do more than take note of this problem. They are still puffed up with the notion that it will solve itself and that, if they wait, they can take full credit for its solution. Not until 1936 will they realize that unemployment is unavoidable in a machine age. Not until 1940 will they realize that unemployment is not necessarily fatal. After ten years of suffering and perplexity, we may discover that when man tapped the resources of science as a means of energy, humanity achieved its racial ambition—to get something for nothing—and that there is nothing immoral in passing the benefits of this uneconomic transaction down the line until they reach and relieve the victims of a system which believes that the Divine Right of Private Property is the basis of civilized society. Then, some party or some leader will realize that, even though a man can find no machine to hire him, there is no reason why he should suffer in the name of law and order, or starve in the name of economics. When that time comes, we shall be so sick of unemployment that we shall accept the revolutionary idea which ends unemployment, as all really revolutionary ideas are accepted—as a matter of course.

XXI

A Tariff War

B OTH parties talk a lot about the Tariff, but neither
of them will do anything about it and neither of
them can bring to an end the tariff war which is paralyzing foreign trade and confusing political thought in
every country. In practice, every nation adopts the rates
which suit its own interests. The American rates are
higher than most, though not so high as some, and were
adopted by the votes of both political parties. Both before and after its enactment in 1930 other countries
raised their rates with greater rapidity and no less selfish
enthusiasm than has been shown by Congress. The result
has been the gradual development of a world-wide tariff
war.

This tariff war grew out of the World War. Every
nation tried to expand its trade so as to create the financial means to support heavy post-war taxation. The
pressure of the German exports required by the reparations payments compelled most European countries to
put up barriers to prevent the dumping of German
goods. Later on, as Soviet Russia began fighting for exchange to support her foreign purchases under the Five-

Year Plan, new barriers were raised against "Bolshevik dumping." In fact, every nation in the world is dumping, or selling its goods at less than cost. The little European powers had all been taught by the British naval blockade that it is very dangerous to become dependent in peace time on international trade and every European country tried to make itself self-supporting, as an insurance of national survival. The British themselves found that they had partly lost their old markets to American and Japanese competition and began to seek, for the first time in generations, a special and privileged trade position which shrank from open competition. Shaky or depreciated money systems, which debased the cost of foreign goods, added the element of sheer fourth-dimensional insanity to international trade. The result has been that every considerable country has raised its tariff rates again and again, and will keep on doing so for some time to come.

The tariff war began in Europe before we ever raised our rates and will continue even after we have reduced our schedules. So long as the fear of war and the burden of debt hang over the nations it will continue. In Europe, the drift towards an economic union has been temporarily checked by the French objection to a customs union between Germany and Austria, although the new British tariff and common anger at the American war-debt policy may give it a new popularity. The nations of the British Empire are working towards an elaborate, but unstable, set of preferences among themselves and aspire to build a tariff wall around the Empire and to promote freer trade among the British peoples. The Soviet Government has married foreign trade to foreign policy so successfully that it has frightened several nations into retaliation but appears sure to dominate Central Asia and the Near East with cheap mass production. International trade has broken down and the British are openly advocating a system of boycotts and barter—disguised as "Buy British" and "Buy from those who buy from us" propaganda—while the Federal Farm Board has used its government credit to sell wheat wholesale in foreign markets. The whole world is slowly moving towards larger economic units, with the distinct possibility that another fifty years may witness a European Customs Union, a British Empire Union, a Pan-American Customs Union and a Soviet-Far Eastern Union.

In the face of this great movement the gestures of American politics are futile and insignificant. Whether we fight with bribes or with cudgels, we shall have to take part in this war. Whether Democrats or Republicans determine our tariff policy, the main lines of that policy are clearly marked. We are working towards a new sort of protection, in which our raw materials are to be protected while our manufactured products take a chance. This shift from our traditional policy, of protection for industries and free trade in raw materials, has already thrown both political parties into such confusion that neither is capable of a clear-cut tariff revision. It began with the agricultural duties of the Act of 1922, expanded with the extensive protection for raw materials granted by the Act of 1930, while the near future will see a tariff on copper or oil or both.

The Democrats are no longer the low-tariff group in this country. The low-tariff men now include Republican bankers who want freer imports so that foreign debtors may be able to make good on American loans. They include Republican industries such as the automobile manufacturers who do not shrink from foreign competition and who hope to trade lower American duties on foreign goods for lower foreign duties on American automobiles. They include the commercial and shipping and transportation interests which make their profits from the exchange, rather than the production, of wealth. And finally, they include the economists and college professors who were taught for years that the British free-trade idea was best for everyone in the long run and who do not yet realize that the British have themselves abandoned free trade.

The new high-tariff group is no longer exclusively Republican. Its mainstay is the farmer: the Republican wheat growers, the Democratic cotton planters, the wool gatherers, sugar producers, orchardists, lumbermen, cattlemen, dairy farmers, coal miners, and all that huge section of our people engaged in the production of

228

food and raw materials. The successful demand for a tariff on cotton—our greatest single export—in the last Act indicates that the object of the new high-tariff party will be to prevent the demoralization of the domestic prices of American raw materials rather than to gouge the consumer. The small and less efficient manufacturers still cling to the protection which the big industrialists are rapidly abandoning. The labor unions, whose wage scale depends on a protected standard of living, are strong for protection. And the rank and file of politicians—to whom the tariff opens a golden opportunity for demanding campaign contributions—are still eloquent for protection, at least so far as their own states are concerned.

This means that the trend in the United States will be first towards a complete protection of every manufactured and raw material, characterized by a gradual reduction in the industrial rates and a gradual increase in the tariff on food. Eventually, it will lead to a situation in which the products of our machinery receive and require no protection at all, while the products of our labor, especially of labor on farms and in mines, will receive complete protection from foreign competition. In other words, protection will be granted on the basis of voting strength. The farmer-labor group will get protection, the bankers and the machines will get free trade. We shall probably reach that stage in twenty years, so the political parties will have plenty of time to get used to the idea.

As a result, there is a fair chance that the Tariff will be taken out of politics, at least out of interparty politics. When protection is given to the masses exclusively it will be suicide for either party to oppose it. Neither party could stand the geographical or mental strain of scampering around the country in pursuit of a constantly shifting interest in tariff protection. So far as the tariff war is concerned, the Democrats will be inclined to buy off our opponents by soft words and bargaining, while the Republicans will tend to use threats and retaliation against foreign attacks on American trade. At home, both parties are so frightened by the result of the last revision that neither one dares do anything about it in the near future.

Hence the election of 1932, for all of the political ballyhooey, will not lead to any great change in the present system. If the Republicans win, the Tariff Commission and the President may get more power; if the Democrats win, the rates on a few products manufactured in stubbornly Republican regions may be reduced and the Tariff Commission may get wider authority. Either way will produce a little loudly advertised tinkering and no real reduction.

It won't make a particle of difference to the world's tariff war. Everybody will still try to get ahead of everybody else, and where treaties or laws stand in the way, every nation will try to get around those treaties and laws, by barter, by special credit arrangements, by the construction of branch factories or by the use of foreign investments. And the United States will be pushed on and on towards a customs union either with the Latin-American countries or with the British Empire or eventually with both. But none of these developments is within the range of practical politics at the present time. The British Empire is still engaged in trying out its own system and unless that system fails to work, we have no grounds for expecting our obvious interest in the Empire to develop into anything like a silent partnership. We already give great facilities to the trade of the Latin-American countries, always excepting the Argentine, and a fat lot of good it has done them. We can only play a waiting game and see whether Europe can unite in the face of Russia, America and the British Empire. If that happens, it will be time enough to consider our next step.

What is happening now is much bigger than any one country and much more important than the fiscal ideas of any President. The whole world is being forced, against its will, into larger units and broader policies, and we are, after all, not a very large part of the world. What will probably happen, so far as we are concerned, is that, as the tariff is taken out of party politics it will be put into our foreign policy. Should that happen, another twenty years should find us facing a brand-new sort of world with the wrong branch of our government in charge of our tariff. What will happen to us and to our trade then will be very painful, but it will do us little permanent harm. After that, we shall have to fend for ourselves with a group of customs unions each of which will be larger and more populous than the United States. By that time, we can afford to let our grandchildren start worrying about the situation. It is enough for us that the election of 1932 won't make the slightest difference to the final result.

XXII

World Power

WHETHER Herbert Hoover, Franklin Roosevelt or some as yet unlocated imaginary point at the center of either political party takes the oath of office on March 4, 1933, the United States will continue to enjoy the advantages and risks of power, together with the other great nations of the earth.

We are approaching the struggles of the twentieth century in a state of diplomatic isolation and we shall no doubt try to play a lone hand in the approaching crisis in world politics. There are war clouds over both Europe and Asia, but, while prophecies of "the next war" are plentiful, it may not come as soon as some people fear or take the form expected. Even as our pacifists urge us to throw overboard our national traditions in order to prevent the coming conflict, the ugly suspicion arises that perhaps we don't really want to stop it. At the outbreak of the Japanese adventure in Manchuria, in the fall of 1931, when it seemed that Russia might be drawn into hostilities, many of us began to speculate as to the effect of a war in Asia on the price of wheat and steel, while statesmen wondered whether a Japan which was entangled in Asia would be less of a "menace" to our Pacific possessions and whether Russian propaganda could be crippled by a new Russo-Japanese set-to. And when the Chinese armies stood off the Japanese for a month of heavy fighting at Shanghai, the old popular appetite for blood cropped up in our headlines, as strong and unregenerate as ever. In the same way, the European crisis raised the thought that a distracted Europe could not be a serious political menace or commercial rival to the United States. Even the money troubles of Great Britain caused us to consider the advantages of being the principal nation to maintain a stable currency. In other words, we are beginning to wonder whether the Old World's peril is not the New World's opportunity, a dangerous thought, inasmuch as we are ourselves in danger and will create as many opportunities here as we find abroad.

Once more we see the nations lining up for the next play, the despoiled against the victors, the nations with the empty pockets against those with the loot, the people in the dark against those with a place in the sun. Germany, Austria, Hungary, Bulgaria, Turkey, Russia, Italy and—perhaps—Japan, confront the nations which won the war and are now so piously devoted to making another war impossible: France, England, Poland, Czechoslovakia, Jugoslavia, Roumania, the Baltic States and—possibly—the United States. Only the British navy, the French army and the barricades of gold and paper stand between the world and a new clash of hostile alliances. So far, these barricades have held and all assaults on the Peace Treaties have collapsed, but the victors are growing older and weaker, the vanquished more confident and more desperate. Sooner or later there may be an explosion. Such is the old-fashioned war scare which the modern world is trying to charm away by disarmament conferences and Peace Pacts, as a wart is charmed away by rubbing it with a piece of raw potato.

The real war scare is one which cannot be charmed away—the threat of social revolution, the war of the poor and ignorant and dispossessed against the rich and educated and powerful, the war for which the Marxians of Moscow hope and work. This war makes armies and navies useless, silences artillery and cripples aircraft, not by missiles but by ideas. War of this sort is the haunting fear of every Old World government. In Japan, it is freely believed that, should the army have to withdraw from China, there would be a revolution. Moreover, while the invasion of Manchuria and a final victory at Shanghai prevent unrest in Tokyo, they create an ideal opportunity for Communist propaganda in China. Germany has stood face to face with the threat of revolution since 1930. The British Empire is putting down Indian sedition with a strong hand, but for the first time in more than a century the British navy experienced mutiny in the summer of 1931, when the rate of pay was reduced. France has had to put down

Communist mutinies in her army, her navy and her colonies. Spain is in a revolutionary twilight which may bring forth communism, chaos or complete reaction. South and Central America are going through a cycle of revolts. In the United States, the pressure of poverty against property is becoming acute, and the debtors are threatening their creditors with repudiation and default.

While we are eagerly laying the ghost of international war and singing loud and cheerful hymns to international peace, we may find ourselves faced with war of an altogether different type. Revolutions may break out in a score of countries. Our foreign loans may be repudiated, our property confiscated, and our citizens imprisoned or lynched on a wide scale. The unofficial business empire which we have built up by the labor of generations may be swept away in a world-wide wave of social revolution, and we may find ourselves struggling to defend our heritage against determined attacks from abroad and critical assaults from our own people.

For this reason, world disarmament is entirely beside the point. The price of world peace has very little to do with scrapping battleships or demobilizing battalions. The world could get rid of international war tomorrow if it would reduce, not its armaments, but its tariffs; repeal, not its military legislation, but its immigration laws; cancel, not its naval programs, but all of its international debts; and surrender, not its legal power to de-

clare war, but its national sovereignties. The price of
political peace is political union, and if we really wish
to ensure a lasting peace, we should work, not for the
outlawry of war or of armaments, but for the outlawry
of the narrow national policies of which war is not the
instrument but the result.

Even a college professor knows that we are not prepared to do anything of the sort; even a retired rear
admiral would admit that we may be too late to do anything to postpone even the type of international war
which is least likely to occur. We lost our best chance to
make peace in 1919, when Wilson was too weak to
block an unsportsmanlike settlement in Europe. A dozen
bitter quarrels—such as the Polish Corridor—arise very
largely from the fact that Woodrow Wilson had his eyes
fixed so firmly on the League of Nations that he turned
thumbs down on the conquered and left them to the
tender mercies of their hereditary enemies. Even at a
time when we had the ships, the men and the money, too,
we were not wise enough to see that substantial justice
was done and to refuse further part in peace policies
which were breeding new wars. If we failed then, is it
likely we would succeed now?

Even so, in 1928, we had one last chance to promote
a real European settlement before the present bitterness
arose. We wasted it in a diplomatic petting party,
known as the Kellogg Pact, while our bankers were tying
Germany up in double bowknots for the next sixty

years and while we were making high-priced whoopee in Wall Street. If we had used one-tenth of the passion we put into the election of Herbert Hoover in backing up our navy, and if we had put one-twentieth of the enthusiasm we lavished on investment trusts, in working for a new deal in Europe, we might have checked disaster even then.

Now it appears too late. Hitler has appeared in Germany and Spain has staged the first major European revolution since 1918. Japan has cast the iron dice over China and, after ten years of conferences in which we agreed to sink our battleships, we must consider the construction of 120 new warships in the next ten years. France has suddenly begun to act like pre-war Germany and an international tariff war has broken out on a world-wide scale, while Great Britain has abandoned the gold standard and everybody is scrambling for gold. The war debts are whipping up European anger against us, and international repudiation, on a scale far greater than that of the Russian Revolution, is in the air.

We are fighting for survival right now. Our means of defense are fairly reassuring. First of all, we have our money. We have five billion dollars of gold—half the monetary gold in the world—and our credit is still unshaken. Money, of course, is not everything, but it is not to be despised. We seem to be developing a pretty steady national character. The fact that we have taken our hardships so quietly proves that. Our government

WORLD POWER

has already survived two great political upheavals. In
1828, the farmers, frontiersmen and riffraff under Andrew Jackson wrenched government away from the
merchants, bankers and gentlemen of the East. In 1860,
the farmers of the West and the manufacturers of the
North seized the government from the grip of the
bankers of the East and the planters of the South. In the
twenty years after 1900 we quietly accepted practically
all of the semi-socialistic proposals of the Populists who
were regarded as dangerous revolutionaries from 1890
to 1900. We are capable of another popular uprising
which may transfer control of government from the
chambers of commerce to—say—the labor unions, without destroying our political institutions. In a world of
brittle governments, where the Ogpu guards the Soviets
against counter-revolution, where Fascist Militia keep
watch over the new order in Italy, and where armies of
semi-military police are necessary to prevent political
violence, our slipshod social discipline may not cut a
very dashing figure but it does symbolize our naïve belief
that we can take revolutions in our stride. And, finally,
we have economic strength of a very high order. Figures
and percentages mean very little, but we produce or
purchase such a large part of the world's output of
wheat, cotton, coal, oil, steel, iron, copper, silver, zinc,
lead, rubber, coffee, cocoa, silk, wool, water power,
horse power and manufactured articles, that our with-
drawal from world trade would spread ruin in a dozen

239

WHAT WE ARE ABOUT TO RECEIVE

other countries, while we are in a position to meet all of our own requirements, if necessary.

As the misfortunes of other nations create opportunities abroad and as our own troubles create unrest at home, we may be tempted to use this power to our own advantage, by adopting what is known as "a spirited foreign policy." When things get bad at home, it is always good politics to start the bands playing and the troops marching, especially if you can pick someone weaker than yourself to fight and can make sure that any fighting will take place somewhere else.

The tap of the drum and the squeal of the fife has drowned the mutter of discontent before this. We would not have fought our war with Spain in 1898 if we had not had a panic in 1893 followed by hard times which lasted right up to the sinking of the *Maine* in Havana harbor. One of the easiest moves in the great game of politics is to substitute imperialism for reform and military glory for an intelligent solution of the unemployment problem.

Moreover, whichever party wins this election will find that the country is in a new mood of nationalism and may sooner or later be tempted to adopt a more aggressive attitude towards other nations. This mood will probably last, with epileptic fits of self-righteous pacifistic Holy Rolling, until about 1940, when the European situation will have cleared up and we shall have begun to master our own economic difficulties. What trouble we may cause, in the meantime, it is difficult to guess. If the Democrats get and keep control, our pressure will be mainly southeastward, directed against Mexico, the Caribbean countries and Central America. If the Republicans are in power, our pressure will be directed against Europe and Asia. Whichever party is in office, it may safely be assumed that we shall do our utmost to preserve peace with every country big enough to defend itself, and shall continue to believe that we are so pure and so strong that we can get world power without fighting for it.

After it is all over and we sober down once more, whether or not we have to fight for what we possess and what we want, we shall discover that the human race has a strong habit of surviving all disasters and coming up bigger and better than ever. Although the world is always shouting that it is going to the devil, the fact is that it has already done so and finds the devil so much less black than expected that it can't believe it is in Hell. The world has, in fact, been having a terrible time since the dawn of history. We are always counting ourselves down and out, then coming back and asking for more. Russia—after a terribly unsuccessful foreign war, a bloody and destructive revolution, loss of her territories, foreign intervention, civil war, chaos, famine, plague and crazy economics—is stronger and more populous than in 1914. China has been in constant revolution since 1911, has been humiliated, disorganized, invaded, wrecked by famines, floods and bandits, and yet the Chinese are more numerous and irritating than ever and are slowly modernizing their government. Germany, beaten in the greatest war of modern times, bled white, dismembered and burdened with debt by her conquerors, has become a great power again within less than a generation of her defeat. In every country, living standards for the masses have soared far above the standards which existed before the most destructive war in history.

We shall survive and the world will survive, no matter who is elected President of the United States on November 8, 1932. A hundred years from now our race will still be here, the petty problems of today forgotten, our ridiculous worries over taxation and prosperity rendered insignificant by the march of science and the progress of human events. To paraphrase Macaulay, sources of energy which are still unimagined, machines not dreamed of by inventors yet unborn, laws not even suspected by our wisest legislators, and new ways of thought and standards of conduct which will regard our most profound statesmanship as childish, will reduce our present miseries and triumphs to a chapter, then to a paragraph, and finally to a footnote in history.

Future schoolchildren may be compelled to memorize the name—together with those of our other presidents —of the man whom we elect in 1932; it is doubtful, nonetheless, that in 2032 more than one educated man out of a hundred will be able to state, offhand, what he accomplished in office or what his election signified. For we are still too young to have learned the only lesson of history, which is that politics, though lots of fun, is only the result and not the cause of human progress.